SOPRANOS ARE **NOT** PIANOS

How Vocal Magic Happens For Women Singers

Ahdda Shur

The Raymond Aaron Group
Markham, Ontario
Canada

BOOK CATEGORY: NON-FICTION

Sopranos Are Not Pianos
How Vocal Magic Happens For Women Singers

By Ahdda Shur

Copyright © 2015 AHDDA SHUR. ALL RIGHTS RESERVED.
info@shurvoice.com
www.shurvoice.com

ALL RIGHTS RESERVED. No part of this work may be reproduced, copied or stored in an informational retrieval system, without express written permission, except in the case of brief quotations embodied in critical articles or reviews.

ISBN #: 978-1-928155-72-0

Photos: Anthony Sansotta

First Edition 2016

PUBLISHED BY:
10-10-10 Publishing,
A division of Raymond Aaron Group™
MARKHAM, ON
CANADA

Address: Raymond Aaron Group
2-9225 Leslie Street
Richmond Hill, Ontario
Canada

SOPRANOS ARE **NOT** PIANOS

How Vocal Magic Happens For Women Singers

CONTENTS

Forward by Raymond Aaron
Thanks and Acknowledgements

Introduction: Women Who Choose to Sing   1

1 Understanding Your Vocal Gift   3

2 Owning the Stage with Real Singing   13

3 Singing with Our Ears   18

4 Sopranos Slide, Piano Keys Hit   25

5 Mental Commands & Breath Control   31

6 Magic Microphone in My Head   39

7 Sound Waves, Vowel Shapes and Resonance   45

8 You Never Can Tell!   51
   Surprising Outcomes
   How a Teen Girl's Efforts Paid Off

9 The Singing Body   57
   Warm-ups for Ease and Power
   A Music Teacher Can Sing Again

10 Words, Words, Words   66

11 Moving Parts: Vowels and Glides   71

12 Keep Your Vocal Capital	75
13 The Sweet Power of High Notes	80
14 Why Opera?	87
15 Your Money Notes	92

16 When Pop Meets Bel Canto
    Healthy Vocal Function
    How a Pop Singer Got Her Voice Back
	99

17 What Can I Do About My Tense Jaw?	105
18 Challenges & Choices	110
Closing Thoughts: The Song Within	119
Recommended Reading List	122
About the Author	124
Testimonials	

FOREWORD

Sopranos Are Not Pianos is an insightful guide for female singers, beginners and professionals alike, who want to learn the foundation of great singing. This book offers a straightforward, easy to understand approach to teaching what could otherwise be a confusing and frustrating subject. The information, advice and several free bonuses in this book are designed to save you from costly detours and delays in your vocal development and career goals.

As an entrepreneur and teacher, I know that it takes practice and the right resources to achieve mastery in any field. By reading this book, the talented and motivated vocalist will discover how to develop her vocal and musical talents, conserve her vocal powers for years, practice with effective power, and handle the pressures and strain of a singing career.

As a publisher, I am pleased to welcome Ahdda Shur into our library of outstanding experts dedicated to helping others achieve success in personal or business fields. It is our hope that this book will help the aspiring singer to save time and money on their path to vocal success.

Raymond Aaron
New York Times Best-Selling Author

THANKS AND AKNOWLEDGEMENTS

To those who made my debut as an author possible: Raymond Aaron for the inspiration to write this book; my talented family, especially Limore Shur for his support and the book's cover design along with Michael and Carolyn Niemann for their editing help; my colleagues Sofia Ames for final proofing and Silvia Berglas for her input; my dear friend, coloratura soprano, Donna Lundeen, for reading earlier drafts and her supportive comments—*Thank You* all. A special thanks to my mother, Nitza, and my daughter, Zahava, for their patience while I labored over chapter headings, syntax and everything else.

A Grand Opera thanks to my beloved voice teachers: the great Romanian/Italian soprano and *Bel Canto* specialist, *Virginia Zeani*, with whom I studied voice at the Indiana University, School of Music, Bloomington; the late *Elisabeth Parham*, my undergraduate teacher at California State University, Northridge, an expert vocal pedagogue and master of English diction, and to *Karl Resnick*, director of the Musical Arts Center of Cincinnati, Ohio, for his belief in me and expertise about vocal function.

Special acknowledgements as well to *Dr. Padovani*, of Zurich, Switzerland, for the vocal therapies he taught me; *Paul Maduale*, Director and Founder of the *Listening Centre* in Toronto, Canada, for the time I spent at his center, experiencing *Alfred Tomatis's* ear/voice methods, and to mezzo-soprano opera soloist, *Béatrice Burley*, whose workshops on Alfred Tomatis's Voice/Ear corrections in Fribourg, Switzerland were so enlightening to me.

Finally, a profound thanks to all my voice students, past, present and future—keep on singing!

Introduction:

Women Who Choose To Sing

Throughout the ages, people have expressed their joys and sorrows through song. A talented singer can touch the heart and inspire the soul. Singing as a community can unite us in the determination to overcome obstacles, console us in times of sorrow, or uplift us during religious worship.

A real element of magic is involved in the singing process. Mastering this intriguing dimension of vocal art requires dedication, musical studies and expert guidance. A beautiful, expressive singing voice, especially when heard live without a microphone, can literally improve the function of our bodies' cells. The particular vibration of sound created by the emotions, breath, and voice of a singer can affect us deeply or not. Some singers have expressive force when they perform, but little voice. Others possess a strong voice but lack emotive power. A rare few, however, have it all: a great voice, charisma, and soulful feeling — and these special artists we make into demigods.

Today's global media and the commercialization of music put tremendous pressure on talented, young female singers to sound and look a certain way. These pre-packaged ideals, created by multi-national companies for music that sells, are often at odds with what is best for a woman's unique vocal abilities and personality. Whether singing classical or contemporary music, in the pressure to earn money, make an impression and get noticed, a talented woman starting out in a promising career can get lost, crash and burn within a few years.

Women who choose to sing feel compelled to do so. They believe they have something to say. For some, this may lead to having lives that are far from ordinary. Choosing to become a singer comes with a certain amount of risk. Therefore, I'm passionate about empowering women singers to find their optimum voice for a lifetime.

Teaching is also an art. I discovered a talent for it early in my international career as an opera singer. In this book, you will find bonus materials, exercises, and stories about women whose voices and lives were dramatically improved using some of my holistic vocal methods.

Whether your vocal gift is great or small, mastering it will take courage, patience and study. Becoming a vocal magician may bring you fame, wealth, and personal fulfillment, or it may lead you down the paths of self-destruction. It's up to you. The magic is within you. To discover how to access it, the right effort is needed. If you want to reach that goal safely, find an expert guide who knows the way.

CHAPTER 1

Understanding Your Vocal Gift

If I were to ask you who was one of your favorite female singers, whom would you pick? Your answer might be very different from mine. However, we would probably agree that many of the women singers we most admire have a distinct sound all their own.

Are you a mezzo-soprano, soprano, alto, contralto, or don't know yet what category fits your voice? Are you already in a musical career or planning for one? Do you perform contemporary or classical music, or write your own music? These are the kinds of questions and answers that come up the more you sing and study. Therefore, having an understanding of your vocal gifts is important.

When you make the effort to learn about your voice, you discover a lot about yourself. No singer is alike. Every female singer comes with her own sound and personality. A good voice teacher recognizes this and can help to enhance your voice and talent.

Many woman singers prefer studying with a teacher who has a similar voice type to their own, or is experienced in training female voices. In my twenty years of teaching hundreds of students on several continents, my specialty has been empowering women to develop their optimum voice and musical style. My own voice type began as a dramatic lyric soprano, however, during my international opera career; I switched to being a mezzo-soprano, performing in a variety of roles as well as in some soprano roles.

The media as well as popular talent shows perpetuate the myth that all you need for singing is an abundance of natural talent. While having a gift for singing is important, those singers that are truly perfect by nature are rare. To sing well at any level, even for those that are exceptionally talented, requires musical coaching, intelligence, skill and a lot more work than most people realize.

While some young female singers may start out with exciting voices and fiery potential, quickly getting noticed and launched into a career, they may often burn out just as fast. The complexities of the music business and the fragile nature of singing contribute to this. Due to the many factors involved, one thing is clear: if you want to perform and sing consistently well, it will take a commitment to several years of studies to master your vocal instrument. Your voice needs time along with proper guidance to mature and blossom correctly. Rushing this process isn't a good idea.

How early should vocal training begin? I get asked this quite often. A young girl's voice changes in puberty but not as dramatically as a boy's voice. Serious vocal training with intensive vocal building shouldn't begin before then, but can safely start around the age of 13 or 14. Until that time, a young girl should learn vocal fundamentals, musical skills and songs that are appropriate for her age. When she enters her twenties, her voice usually changes again, becoming fuller and richer. Vocal range and tone may modify several times, especially as we get older. When these developments occur, we may need to make adjustments to our repertoire and technique.

Being a successful singer requires having discipline similar to those who train as athletes. Whether you are a professional singer, a student in high school or a member of a choir, your overall health affects your voice. Therefore, if you want to sing well for many years, leading a healthy lifestyle is crucial. Any heavy smoking and drinking, or singing while seriously ill or with inflamed vocal cords should be avoided at all times.

The vocal cords can also be negatively compromised from common mistakes such as over-singing, speaking with too much tension in the throat, singing with an imperfect technique, or in a musical style, that doesn't fit your vocal abilities. The good news is that with proper care and a solid vocal method, you should be able to sing with a healthy and usable voice well into your sixties, or longer.

Our sound and self-image

Our voice emerges from our innermost being during the first few days of our time here on earth. We cry, we scream, we shout, we moan, we yell. We begin to babble making silly sounds. We listen—to various sounds around our homes, to the sounds of nature, the wind, the cat, the dog. We imitate what we hear. We imitate our parent's voices, our sibling's voices. Then, in elementary school, we may already be singing or just talking a lot! We start getting positive or negative feedback about our voice from other people. Sometimes we hear people say things like, *"What a beautiful voice you have;"* *"Oh, you are so musical!"* Or, *"You are so talented."* Some of us may hear other comments such as, *"You always sing too loudly!"* Or, *"Tone it down."* If we are extroverts, we may hear this phrase quite often: *"You talk too loud,"* *"Be quiet"* or, *"Please don't sing, you are off-key!"* And then, for those delightful kids who just can't stop, *"Please...stop singing so much, you're driving us all crazy!"*

What starts out in life as a joyful expression from our heart (whether we sing well or not) can become overcast by these kinds of reactions and opinions from other people. We singers can be particularly sensitive to criticism because our voice is such an important part of us. It's our sound identity. This is a crucial and important thing to understand. Our voice suddenly becomes an object, something outside of ourselves. This may cause us to doubt ourselves or push too hard to perfect our singing and our voice. In that effort, we may overdo things and find ourselves off balance, physically and mentally.

The efforts and obligations to sustain a musical career can also affect us. The need to perform and measure up to standards can become a strain, taking the initial fun and joy out of singing. I know quite a few famous opera singers who have shared how they love to sing, but have grown weary of the business of singing. We also encounter daily stresses and tensions from our various obligations at home, at work and striving to achieve our goals. Running around doing our errands or just being stuck in a lot of traffic, can easily get us stressed out. We forget to breathe, to play, to laugh.

If you're feeling stressed or anxious, immediately tensions occur in your body and in your voice. Therefore I give my voice students, whether they are beginners or professional singers, daily mind/body exercises for better posture, vocal function, and breath control. These methods also keep the voice healthy and strong. Having been an international opera singer, I know from personal experience and from interacting with many professional singers, how unresolved stress in the body and mind can negatively impact singing.

Let's go back to the first question of what kind of female voice type you have. Are you a soprano, mezzo-soprano, alto or contralto? Are you still finding that out, or changing from one voice type to another?

Sometimes, students arrive at my voice studio firmly believing they are altos, when they are actually sopranos. Or the opposite occurs. Either way, taking voice lessons will give you better insights as to where your voice functions fluently, and how to strengthen the weaker areas.

Studying with a teacher who had a singing career (or still does) is very helpful. It's even better if she still has a good voice to demonstrate for you. It's much easier to understand how something should be done by observing and listening to how your teacher sings a phrase, scale pattern, or creates different vocal colors or other expressive devices. An experienced teacher should also help you identify the right singing sensations that you must acquire, in order to perform on a consistently good level. She should help guide you when selecting repertoire that best fits your personality, musical and vocal abilities. These are all crucial aspects to vocal training.

Getting help for sudden or ongoing vocal problems

In the maintenance and development of your natural gifts, you want to have a select team of trusted and respected advisors who know your voice, helping you to stay on track. In addition, you must learn how to be calm and objective about your singing! Learn how to analyze your sound and your vocal faults so that you can self-correct. Naturally, if you become very ill or develop some sudden or ongoing vocal problems, you should get the professional or medical help that you need as soon as possible.

This is what happened to me. In my early thirties, after singing professionally for 10 years, and earning a Master's degree in Opera, I made my European operatic debut. Soon after, I suddenly got ill with a bad flu, which affected my singing. My voice shut down. Determined to overcome this, I searched for help. Fortunately, I encountered a brilliant ENT (ear, nose and throat) doctor who not only helped my vocal cords, but also specialized in vocal therapies for reconditioning the voice (I write more about this in the chapter, *Your Vocal Capital*). This led me to study further about vocal function, sound and energy healing. These experiences became part of my holistic vocal methods: *Bel Canto with VOGA™ voiceyoga for peak performances*.

When there are ongoing issues with breath control or vocal function, it is unrealistic and self-defeating to expect significant vocal transformation to occur overnight. It takes patience, courage and time to retrain the muscles and the mind. My *Shurvoice* students usually experience a noticeable improvement in breath and vocal function within the first four to six months of weekly 60-minute lessons. Even without major vocal problems to correct, it may take several years of study just to know how to practice effectively and how to hear yourself properly.

To facilitate learning, I encourage students to record their voice lessons and practice with the recording during the week. Along with lessons, many of my students use my Audio CD: *VOGA*™ *voiceyoga for peak performances, Warm-ups in 9 minutes or less!* Attending master classes and workshops in a variety of venues is also recommended. Master classes give singers a chance to perform their songs and help the nervous system get used to performing in high stress conditions.

As unnecessary tensions and stresses in your vocal instrument decrease, you are better able to bypass the critical and self-conscious part of yourself. It becomes easier to connect to your emotions, which naturally animates your singing. Paradoxically, the more control you attain, the greater you can let go and trust your instrument. Then the music begins to flow through you directly to the audience. When everything comes together like that, it's an exhilarating feeling.

Attending live concerts

What you feed your ears impacts how good your ear and listening skills can become. To develop fully, the ear needs to receive a wide envelope of frequencies on an ongoing basis. Listening to singers on the radio, on YouTube, iPod or on CDs is excellent, but should be a secondary activity. These should not be a replacement for ongoing exposure to live, unfiltered, acoustic instrumental and vocal singing. In addition, you learn so much from watching live performers, experiencing all of that music directly, fully focused in the moment without distractions.

The process of listening to a melody, remembering the notes and re-sounding them is something worth contemplating. Let's stop and think about it. Just contemplating this idea for a moment can relax your mind. Take a moment right now to focus inward. See if you can hear a song or a melody inside yourself.

What happens when your mind quiets down? Notice how your breathing subtly changes. Your shoulders may feel more relaxed, and your lower ribs expand a bit as the breath comes in. If you sing a phrase now, what happens?

Feeling, Concentration and Imagination

After you have defined your voice type and range, you begin to select the best repertoire and musical genres that fit your voice and your personality. Is your voice and talent best suited for classical music, folk, pop or jazz? Sometimes it takes several years of study before you can decide. Your voice teacher is usually an important and crucial part of this process.

Once you've selected a song, begin contemplating what you are doing with that particular piece of music. What is your purpose for singing this song or that role?

What are your feelings when you hear this music? What do you know about that particular composer's music overall?

When you prepare for an opera or musical theater role, a vocal recital or recording project, create an artistic intention for the piece you will sing. This intention will evolve as you perform the piece or role over time. However, whether studying or performing a musical work, having an intention helps to focus your feeling and imagination. These intangible qualities are important. They fuel your ability to serve the music and its message as written by the composer. Once these artistic qualities are in line, you will also know what kind of music you want to sing and why.

Feeling, concentration and imagination developed and sustained over time, ultimately gives you access to the ability of tuning into a higher level of inspiration. Singing in this way allows you to sing with your heart and soul. Then, your studies take your talent even further. When you sing from this kind of inspired focus and skill, your audience feels it. They connect to you responding to the purity of your focused artistic intention along with your vocal talent.

Below is your first Free Bonus. This is a three page PDF listing of some of my suggested guidelines for repertoire, organized by musical style, age and level.

Free Bonus #1:
www.shurvoice.com/Repertoire-Bonus

CHAPTER 2

Owning the Stage with Real Singing

As a little girl, I was always singing throughout the day. At night, I used to hum myself to sleep. Other times, I'd quietly practice holding a long note that ends a song until I felt it finished just right, not in a feeling of tightness in the throat, but with a little inward motion, a tug at the belly button. The note released effortlessly and I would think — *that's it!* And then I would go through it again, just for the fun of it.

Today I teach some of those early vocal and breathing sensations to others. For me, singing is simply an expression of who I am. Some would say that I was born to sing. I am always practicing parts of arias, songs or scales, because I just love it. Whether I have a concert to prepare or not, I must sing!

Performing a song on stage, with or without a microphone, isn't as easy as professional singers make it look. Real singing — not hyped up, artificially mixed and made in a recording studio—is an art. It requires years of practice, and a big dose of natural talent. This includes having a good musical ear and the ability to learn music easily. Finally, you must have some kind of fire in your belly, a love of music, words and of making some noise!

It's crucial to practice in, and learn how to use, the acoustics in the space you sing in, as a natural feedback system. Merely singing softly into a microphone is not going to develop your voice. To sing well, you must first know how it feels to project your voice in a room or in a small hall, if you want to sing well. Gradually, you build stamina and power in order to be heard in bigger venues.

Talented singers should not only learn to sing with ease and power (with or without amplification), but also own the stage when they sing. They must move an audience with the ease and beauty of their voice, musicality, phrasing and expression. When I work with aspiring young singers, I encourage them to be musically and artistically smart. To be successful in your singing life requires more intelligence than people realize.

IPod, Cloud Music Libraries, and Vocal Training

We live in a time when a young teen singer has a pocket library of countless new songs downloaded from iTunes or YouTube videos. Young people today can feel rather egocentric about their music, but usually have little musical training to back up their opinion.

Kids today are rich in technologically well-produced music, but they are poor when it comes to hearing singers perform live, with or without a microphone. It's becoming more difficult these days for young people to experience a beautiful and resonant voice that is unmixed and unplugged. Many times the only place this happens on a regular basis is in places of religious worship, concert halls or in opera houses.

Remember, you're never going to sound like your favorite recording artist. You can try to copy and paste, but it won't take you very far! Every voice is different, and every singer has different talents. All the great pop and jazz singers tailor their songs to suit their range and abilities. They sing in the best keys for their voices and also have great musical skills. The two go together.

Benefits of musical education early in life

Parents of young teens often don't understand how much time or musical training is required for singing. Having students take voice lessons in high school is an excellent foundation for further studies into their college years, as well as giving female teens more confidence in their overall communication skills and poise. Most teen girls' voices will not really mature until their mid-twenties.

Over the past 10 years, I've seen a drastic decline in the most basic of musical education for young people.

I've had young teens showing up for their first voice lessons expecting to sing their favorite artist's songs in a matter of weeks, never having sung a scale or knowing anything about music! Yes, there is something called "auto-tune" recording software today. However, let's get real about vocal training. If you went to a piano teacher, wouldn't you expect to learn scales, chords, read music and be told to practice daily? Singers should learn basic musical skills; know how to read music and learn scale patterns called *vocalizes*. These are a variety of scale and melodic patterns that build the voice and musical skills.

Training for the musical ear should ideally begin at birth and continue daily. A young child should hear music that is varied in styles and complexity, performed by expert singers and musicians. Good singing should be heard in the home, at school, in religious organizations, and informally whenever possible.

Singing in choirs or school shows is best suited for those students who not only have a pleasing voice but also an above average musical ear. The better one's natural voice is—a pleasing tone, singing easily on pitch and clear diction, sufficient power and range—the better one's chances of succeeding in vocal studies or having a career in music.

With today's excellent musical resources, students and professional singers can practice their music at home using vocal music books that also come with piano or orchestra accompaniment tracks. You must learn the accompaniment to your songs along with your own part. Singers don't usually sing all by themselves! Begin building your personal library of music, one or two books at a time.

Practicing with orchestra tracks is very helpful for intermediate and advanced students. In general, piano tracks are easier to follow than orchestra tracks, particularly for beginning students. I highly recommend taking advantage of these resources. Of course, you must remember that ideally, the orchestra or piano follows you, and not the other way around. Still, these books give a student a great way of learning exactly what the accompaniment sounds like and what it feels like to sing with an orchestra, piano or jazz combo.

Below, you'll find your second Free Bonus. I've made a three page PDF listing of vocal anthologies ranging from classical and musical theater to jazz and pop songs. These books are ones that I frequently use or recommend to my students. Most of these books also come with excellent full orchestra tracks, jazz combos or piano accompaniment tracks. Some of the orchestra or piano tracks are good enough to perform with, or to use for your accompaniment in an audio or video recording.

FREE BONUS #2:
www.shurvoice.com/MusicBooks-Bonus

CHAPTER 3

Singing with Our Ears

As noted in the previous chapter, it's not enough to have a good voice to become a good singer; you must also have a very developed musical ear. These essential components along with vocal talent are basic requirements needed to sing.

Musical and vocal training depend on the ear and how we listen. Even if you don't have much of a musical ear, studies have shown that classical musical training can improve brain function and has even been found to actually improve the IQ of students.

You are always carrying your instrument inside you. Your voice may be generated by your vocal cords, but it is powered by, and sustained by, your hearing skills, breath and body. We are going to speak more about this in later chapters.

To sing a melody we usually hear it first with our ears. If you can't hear it accurately, you can't sing it.

You listen to and retain the memory of the melody in your mind. Then after hearing it a few times, you sing that phrase back and (hopefully) it's the exact copy of what you heard and recorded inside yourself. Isn't that a magical thing to be able to do? Just realizing this fact can be a liberating contemplation.

For more about the importance of the ear and classical music, I refer you to the studies and methods of the celebrated music educator and vocal therapist, the great French audiologist, Alfred Tomatis. His work influenced many of leading music educators, learning specialists, and voice therapists.

What singers you listen to

In the beginning of your singing life, you admire someone else's singing and their voice. If you are lucky, their voice is similar to yours and you imitate their way of singing. This can be helpful to you. Imitating a clear, expressive and beautiful voice is an ideal way to begin to sing. The more outstanding are the vocal models you listen to, the better. However, if you imitate a singer whose voice is completely different from yours, you may get into some vocal trouble!

Voice students should hear and sing a range of styles: classical, pop, musical theater and folk songs. This develops their voices and musical ear. They should then learn all their songs by heart. A singer must train to memorize hundreds of songs, along with the accompaniment that goes with them. If they want to do musicals or opera, they must memorize complete roles as well. Beginners and young students should be encouraged to learn folk and children's songs, and American popular classic songs that educators and singers designate as the *American Song Book* by composers such as Cole Porter, G. Gershwin, Rodgers and Hammerstein, etc., to develop musical skills and avoid imitating someone currently famous. (See Free Bonus#1 - *Repertoire List*).

My early musical influences

I was born into a musical, singing family and was always singing as a little girl. My late father, the composer Bonia Shur, had a flamboyant personality and was also an expert accordionist, mandolin player and choir director. He would play the piano at home every day and night, composing and singing his choral works. He also brought me along to many of his rehearsals and choral concerts. Later on, he became a well-known composer of contemporary Jewish religious music. My early childhood was spent in Israel. At that time, my mother, Nitza, (now Nitza Niemann) was a concert singer and conductor of an award-winning girls' choir. When we moved to Los Angeles, California, she decided to focus solely on her singing career. As a little girl, I was very proud to attend her many opera performances in Los Angeles as well as hearing her practice at home the exciting works of Verdi, Puccini, Brahms, and other composers' music.

In the mid-1960s, my mother was in demand in Los Angeles for her dramatic flair and exciting mezzo-soprano voice. The acclaimed German soprano, Lotte Lehmann, then living in Santa Barbara, had accepted her into an elite group of opera singers for intensive coaching sessions, as did the highly respected German/Jewish conductor and pianist, Fritz Zweig.

My mom knew that I also loved to sing. When we still lived in Israel, my father had brought me to a nearby Kibbutz, to attend the opera rehearsals he was doing there. He was directing a group of excellent local singers in a production of Mozart's *Die Zauberflöte* (*The Magic Flute*). Although I was only three years old, I came home singing all the arias by heart, enchanted by Mozart's music. (As an adult, I performed the role of Third Lady in a new production of *Die Zauberflöte* at the Zürich Oper, Switzerland. This was a brilliant production directed by the late Jean-Pierre Ponnelle, and conducted by Nicholas Harnoncourt.)

My performing career took off at the age of seven, when I was invited to perform in the children's chorus of a small but thriving opera company in Los Angeles. This came from an inside connection. From whom else, of course, but my mother, Nitza!

My mother had been cast in Verdi's grand opera, *Il Trovatore* (*The Troubadour*), in the fiery mezzo-soprano leading role of Azucena, a tormented gypsy with a terrible secret. Nitza was outstanding in this dramatic mezzo-soprano role and was getting noticed by important opera people for her interpretation. This was before the celebrated tenor Plácido Domingo became General Artistic Director of our current LA Opera Company, transforming Los Angeles into an international opera hub.

This production of Verdi's *Il Trovatore* ran for several performances at the Wilshire Ebell Theater, a prestigious medium size theater in Los Angeles. The children sang in the second act, which opens with the famous *Anvil Chorus,* sung by the Gypsy families and workers. I loved my costume and sang with gusto. Being on stage and hearing the orchestra below, I really got into Verdi's music, acting my part and feeling very happy. I also felt very accomplished. The big reward for my opera debut was an ice cream fudge sundae all for myself, no sharing.

The next year, I got a solo role with another company and even got paid—a grand $20 per performance. This company was doing Puccini's masterful one-act comic opera, *Gianni Schicchi*. In this opera, my mother displayed her comic timing in the role of Zita, and I sang the part of the little boy, Gherardino. That season, we did about fifteen performances of *Gianni Schicchi*.

To learn the music for my part in Verdi's opera (and later for my role in Puccini's opera), my mother trained me in a very natural and simple way. After my little brother, Ophir, and I were comfortably settled for sleep, my mom would sit by our beds and sing Verdi's *Anvil Chorus* with her beautiful and expressive voice. She then taught me the Italian words which I loved saying. We would practice the melody separately and then put the words to it. In this way, I learned my part very easily. I fell asleep with the music still in my head. This is the way children learn in general. Singers do very well with this method as well.

After those introductory lessons at night, we also studied after school. My mother played the music on the piano, and we went over my lines. By the time rehearsals arrived, I was all set. All this showed my mother that I was suited for a musical path. However, she wisely put no pressure on me then; I didn't need to be perfect, just good enough. These early experiences learning music must have also affected me later on, as a teacher. I like to remind my singers that we sing with our ears first, the eyes follow second.

Listening vs. Hearing

Vocal training involves learning how to hear ourselves objectively and in an informed way along with hearing lots of really good singers. Therefore, what you feed your ears impacts how "good" your ear is. Start by taking the ear buds out of your ears! Take a walk in nature; listen to beautiful bird sounds. Attend some classical music concerts. These days this is usually the only way to hear orchestral and vocal music performed without electronic amplification.

We should train the ability to not only sing pitches correctly but also detect differences in quality of sound, timbre, and rhythm. We must be able to sing what we hear, quickly and accurately. The importance of first having a musical ear, and then further training it, cannot be overstated. In vocal lessons, you also learn how to "listen" to your voice in a new way. Additionally, make time to listen to great singers performing in various musical genres. Listen for how much emotion, clarity of tone, timbre and resonance they possess and analyze what it is that you like.

Disturbances in the ear's ability to hear can affect learning and speech. This was discovered by the late Alfred Tomatis (previously mentioned), the author of numerous books, including "*The Conscious Ear*" and the "*The Ear and the Voice.*" Tomatis developed amazing ways to transform a variety of vocal and learning problems with his revolutionary ear and voice therapy programs. His work has transformed the lives of singers and speakers, children with autism, dyslexia, stuttering, and other learning disorders. Tomatis's revolutionary work and techniques with sound frequencies, especially with Mozart's music, and its unique healing effects, heavily influenced the career of music education expert, Don Campbell, famous for his book, "*The Mozart Effect.*"

During my singing career, I was fortunate to study with some of Alfred Tomatis's leading students. These studies increased my understanding of the importance of the ear and its effect on vocal function. It also gave me access to special listening exercises that have dramatically improved many of my students' vocal and musical abilities.

CHAPTER 4

Sopranos Slide, Piano Keys Hit

I use this phrase often in my teaching practice. I hope it makes you laugh! Having a little laugh is relaxing. It makes you feel spontaneous, connected to a place right below your belly button, which is the seat of the breath and the voice.

Singers learn how to sustain sound frequencies from breath, resonance and vibration. We create an acoustical space that supports sound waves. Therefore, we actually train to **contain** vibrations of vowels and consonants. This is done by fine control of a steady stream of air vibrating the skeleton and flowing into the front part of our face, referred to as *"The Mask"* in Italian *Bel Canto* method. (*Bel Canto*, Italian for *Beautiful Singing*.)

Remember, we don't sing from our eyes! We sing first with our ears and our body. It's impossible simply to hit notes in the same way that you see a pianist doing. A pianist has to press the keys on the keyboard to make the notes come out. You have no keys in your throat to press or hit. The vocal cords are in your throat. When functioning healthily they close on the airflow automatically and vibrate, producing notes. You can't get inside to press on them.

If you carry the mental commands such as *hit the note* when you sing, it may backfire on you. If you take this approach without really understanding it, your mind/body connection attempts to respond to this command. However, as you try to hit something, all that may happen is a tightening and squeezing in your throat. Right away, you are in trouble. Your approach interferes with the automatic process of the vocal cords vibrating on the airflow.

Our voice is more like a sliding instrument. Think of a trombone or a violin. These musicians are actually sliding the trombone, or the moving the violin bow on the string, and usually in a straight line. This visual is closer to what happens when we sing. The way our tones are made has nothing to do with hitting anything.

However, most of us learn about singing by sitting or standing near a keyboard or piano. As we look at the keyboard, we automatically begin thinking *Up and Down*. Or we look at the music notes that go up and down. Either way, our eyes take over and the ears get confused.

Looking at the piano, we begin subconsciously to identify with it. Whatever the eyes and mind focus on, they become it. This is an ancient yogic teaching. Subconsciously, we equate the piano's keyboard length with how our voice moves up and down. The high notes seem so high and hard to sing and the low notes equally hard to reach.

In our throat resides our larynx, which houses the vocal cords. The idea of *up and down* caused by looking at a keyboard, creates an unconscious movement up and down in our larynx, similar to when we swallow, which hinders the flow of sound.

We are already at a disadvantage when we sing, since our instrument is inside of us and we don't hear ourselves accurately. If we add to that problem the unconscious perception that this long keyboard is in our throat, we're really in trouble.

A piano's high notes also sound very different from a female voice, having a different aural frequency. These notes possess a thinner timbre (quality of sound) than a female voice, regardless of whether a singer is an alto, mezzo-soprano, or soprano. Never confuse the small bell-like high tones of the piano with the higher part of your own voice.

Most of my students do much better after hearing me demonstrate a high note or phrase, than when listening to it on the piano. When a woman is singing at an octave above middle C and higher, her sound should be fuller, richer and more vibrant than a piano could ever hope to be in that range. Singers learn best through imitating what they hear. Your voice teacher or an expert singer demonstrating how to make a good tone, or how to sing a particular phrase, will often be more helpful than a demonstration on another instrument or mere intellectual analysis.

Though we must accurately hear the music to sing it, intellectual analysis has its place. Additionally, having a good singing technique requires defining what kinds of mental commands work best for you. However, the scope of this book doesn't allow me to go into great depth about mental commands, as this requires a live demonstration (though more about this subject is covered in Chapter 5). When combined with our listening abilities, the art of singing is a magical and mysterious process that no computer has yet been able to do. We really have an amazing power within us. Take a moment now and really contemplate this.

Let's consider a typical performance scenario: you are halfway through singing your aria or musical theater number. Now that climactic end of the song is approaching. You need to hold that long note in the higher part of your voice. You miss, fall, and crumble on it. Every singer can go through this for a variety of reasons. Usually, it occurs when you're not yet established with those higher notes, the right mental commands to make them happen, or in that piece of music.

Female singers, particularly those who study pop, jazz or other contemporary music, tend to suppress the higher part of their voice. They force the lower voice to crank up into the middle and head voice. Over time, this can cause a variety of vocal tensions or physical constrictions, covered in later chapters.

So often, young singers are looking to press something when they sing, especially for the higher notes. It's a mistaken idea in the mind that says, *"I've got to press something to make this sound/word come out."* Since we are *not* pianos, we'll have to find a way to press something that actually *works* for good singing. We have no keys or valves, and we can't get into our throats to make the notes and words come out that way. The mind is trying to get the body and the voice mechanism to do something it simply can't do. Confusion sets in between the mind's ideas about singing, and what actually occurs when singing.

As a first step to get out of this, I sometimes ask my students to move their arms as if conducting while they sing. This is not the traditional idea of standing still with arms at your side, as is often done in choirs. These kinds of gentle arm movements help to free up the breathing system, relaxing the mind to better notice how the voice flows out. Suddenly you feel and sing so much better!

Remember, you're not a piano. Your voice is not fixed. You are creating your instrument throughout your entire life. Yet, just like pianists and other instrumentalists, singers also benefit from practicing scales, *arpeggios*, fast *coloraturas*, *staccato*s and *legato*. However, unlike instrumentalists, building a good voice doesn't require a student to practice scales for hours on end! Your voice teacher helps you to establish practice guidelines appropriate to your level, and how to sing even, accurate, beautiful scale patterns with different vowels, syllables or words. By practicing many kinds of *vocalizes*, you learn, identify and memorize musical patterns you encounter in the songs, musical theater and opera roles that you will master later on.

Beginners should spend between five to fifteen minutes a day doing simple *vocalizes*, gradually building up to thirty minutes a day. However, a singer at any level can safely spend ten to twenty minutes on basic breathing exercises and vocal warm-ups. There is a catch though. It's better to sing a few *vocalizes* correctly, than to do too many *vocalizes* incorrectly.

In addition to practicing daily vocalizes, serious students will need at least 45 to 60 minutes, five days a week, devoted to practicing their songs, memorization, and interpretation. The professional or advanced student may spend up to two hours in any given practice session on technique, repertoire and memorizing music. They must also make time for listening to their music or rehearsing with their accompanist, working on their acting and any other aspects of the songs or roles they will perform.

CHAPTER 5

Mental Commands and Breath Control

Singers must establish simple mental commands to direct their breath, voice and the music they sing. These commands establish control over the entire vocal instrument. Once control is there, the focus can move to **Feeling, Imagination** and **Concentration**.

The classical vocal traditions that I teach offer a holistic approach to the vocal and breathing system. When done correctly, the singer gains power and ease, beautiful diction, *legato* and *staccato* phrasing. This type of breathing system naturally expands the diaphragmatic region, along with a flexible movement felt in the lower abdomen, which co-ordinates the flow of air. The lowest ribs open on a small amount of air (not with outward muscles), but through a subtle impulse of air from within. This action gently opens the intercostal muscles attached to the floating ribs.

When these movements occur, you feel a gentle resistance against the ribs as the sound is emitted, yet nothing should be held rigidly in this area.

When you use a mental command such as *"hold the note,"* particularly for a high note, your body may not understand this at first. The command of *"hold the note"* commonly used by conductors and choir directors often translates imperfectly for the young singer's vocal mechanism. As a result, the singer's body responds by stiffening something.

Stiffening and becoming rigid in our vocal mechanism is never a good thing in singing. The breathing and vocal system should remain elastic, and **flexible.** It's also good to remember not to open the mouth too wide or lower the jaw too far down, when singing. Of course we *do* open the mouth more for higher notes, such as high G, A, B and high C in the upper musical staff. However, in general, using a smaller mouth position allows for better diction and less stress on the muscles of the jaw hinge. It's a position that classically trained singers, particularly those trained in the Italian vocal traditions prefer to use, whenever possible.

When you practice singing a note that is held for several or more beats, try a different mental command. The phrase *"holding the note"* doesn't really mean we hold anything. Rather, what it means is that you are **sustaining** tones and vibrations as the ribs remain slightly open for a specific period of time. Your mind must remain calm to direct the flow of sound. Then, Imagination and Feeling come into play. Use these intangibles to motivate and inspire your breathing. If you want to go beyond mere pretty vocalism and really communicate with an audience, this kind of inner connection to music is essential.

To help students better understand such phrases such as *"support the tone"* and *"sing from the diaphragm,"* or other vocal terms that many singers frequently misunderstand, I use other terms that are more body specific, preferring to keep imagery out of the training process when possible. I also have students explore small movements that improve posture and alignment that help students identify their own optimal breathing process. For example, a student may be guided to adjust the balance of the upper body, pelvic girdle, or both. They may start to notice how using their arms in certain gentle movements, engages the kinesthetic part of their mind, making the act of singing feel easier and more spontaneous.

Exercise of Awareness
Level 1: Move, Breathe and Sing

- Stand tall. Feet are hip-width apart.
- Raise your arms up and bring your hands over your heart, or at the sides of your waist.
- Exhale audibly on the letter "F" in 4 slow beats. Repeat slowly. Feel your upper teeth pressing lightly on your lips as you say "F".

- Now exhale slowly on "F" again, while moving your arms above your waist, as if opening curtains in front of you.
- Move your arms again, as if conducting while releasing a long "F" sound.
- Do the same movements again, singing a descending scale or part of a song.
- Repeat the scale playfully and casually.

Now, try a phrase from your favorite song. Keep the posture elastic and the arms above the waist, moving slightly apart as you sing. How does that feel?

Giving the mind something to focus on that is tangible, such as your arms or hands gently moving while you sing, makes it easier to feel the kinesthetic aspect of your singing. Holding your hands above the waist, elbows slightly extended, may look old fashioned, but it automatically gives your upper body that tiny lift you need for good breath support.

Every singer is different and can hold tension differently. However, there are certain habitual areas where tension accumulates in everyone. This is in the central nervous system, which is powered by the diaphragmatic region. If you are tense or stressed, what usually happens is the breath pulls in, the shoulders hunch over and the voice sinks down.

When your thoracic diaphragm is held tensely, your breath is locked. This affects your thinking as well. The breathing system has to be trained for singing and often needs to be reconditioned. Once this is achieved, you are able to access greater ease and power in your voice, no matter if you sing opera, pop, musical theater, jazz, or folk music. Your vocal technique must be reliable and completely understood both intellectually and kinesthetically. When you sing, you have no time to "think." You need to develop your kinesthetic/feeling awareness of your voice, core body support, intercostal breathing, and phrasing as directed by your musical ear. Intellectual and artistic analysis must be done before and after you sing — but not while you sing. Long before you perform, you must set where you will breathe in a phrase, tempos, dynamics, styling, and so forth.

In performance, your goal is to remain in the present moment. When singing, use simple commands, to better focus on the phrasing and dramatic content of the music. Your technique should serve your artistic Feeling, Imagination and Concentration; qualities that transcend the sound of your voice and help bring the music to life.

Breath control and sound

The study of how to produce optimum resonance referred to in classical singing as placing tones in *"The Mask"* or *"The Dome"* (at the front of the face), is also part of mastering breath control. *The Mask* is covered more fully in Chapter 6. The main thing to understand is that you are a living, breathing and emotional instrument. Never confuse your vocal sound with the piano or the other instruments accompanying your singing. Another good rule to remember is that when your singing doesn't feel physically good to you, or feels overly tight in your throat, it's usually not right.

Here are some of the kinesthetic responses of the body that singers can learn to become aware of and employ while they sing:

- yawn reflex
- sigh reflex
- sneeze reflex
- laugh reflex.
- nostrils gently flaring

You should observe how the incoming air gently expands both sides of your lower ribs right above your waist. It's felt as a subtle elasticity in the intercostal muscles attached to the lower floating ribs. This must first be awakened and then trained. The ribs and intercostal muscles reach into the back along your spine; therefore, we also use our back muscles to some extent.

Along with this, observe the subtle action of the transverse muscle at a center point immediately below the belly button. It moves or bounces, a bit inwards, as the air comes in and out. The movement inwards helps support waves of sound and maintains the balance of the upper torso. This is the seat of vocal support. (Notice that it is slightly below the diaphragmatic region, in the lower abdomen.) It's a light pulsation of in/out, easily felt when gently laughing. This pulsation controls ease of exhalation, supports the emission of tone and helps to regulate the incoming air as well.

It is very liberating to identify and be aware of these subtle movements. This little area should not be confused with the entire lower abdominal area or length of the transverse (girdle) muscle. I like to call this small area, my *Round Pedal*. It should feel like a gentle bouncing in/out, moving incrementally depending on the phrasing. To identify this action, I ask the student energetically to repeat words such as *"No," "Yes,"* or *"Go away,"* while gently placing their hand at that area, to fully notice this pulsation. Words holding emotion easily activate this area.

Part of my training in holistic breathing methods comes from having studied with the celebrated Romanian/Italian soprano, Madame Virginia Zeani. A specialist in the traditions of the authentic Italian *Bel Canto* techniques, she had a long and varied international opera career, spanning lyric coloratura roles to heavier soprano roles. She was known for her beauty, vivid acting, and unique sound. She was especially famous for her distinctive and moving performances of the tragic courtesan, Violetta Valéry, in Verdi's operatic masterpiece *La Traviata*. Zeani also held the record for having sung this extremely challenging soprano role over 600 times all over the world.

After she retired from active performing, Zeani began teaching at the Indiana University School of Music, at Bloomington, Indiana, when I was in graduate school there, earning my degrees in Voice and Opera Stage Direction. Even though she was nearly 60 years old when she began her illustrious tenure at Indiana University, her voice, energy and beauty were as fresh as ever. Though an extraordinary soprano, Virginia Zeani was also an exceptionally gifted teacher. Supportive yet demanding, with high standards for musical and artistic preparation, she made singing seem easy. I was fortunate to have been her student, and loved every minute of my time with her. The incredible charm and force of her personality, along with the depth of her experience in opera was breathtaking.

Zeani imparted to her students not only the joy of singing, but great wisdom about singing from her impressive career and fascinating life. She taught us with such clarity, humor, and musical taste that each lesson has remained as fresh as ever in my mind. Her mentoring and belief in my abilities was not only life changing for me, but also for many of her other talented students who went on to become well-known international opera singers or respected voice teachers.

CHAPTER 6

Magic Microphone in My Head

The art of singing began to change in the last century with the advent of recordings. With the invention of the microphone, the art of singing was changed forever, and sometimes for the worse. Recordings, television shows, competitions, and movies have all greatly transformed how singers perform, and how we hear their voices.

In today's music scene, almost every singer has experienced singing with a microphone. Therefore, we have to take into consideration how this affects our vocal quality. The use of a microphone picks up many flaws, while it also magnifies good vocal qualities. Using a microphone can enhance your sound, as well as distort it. The microphone is essential in places with poor acoustics, open-air venues, parties and other suboptimal sound environments.

However, if you are *relying* on a microphone for vocal quality, or expecting the studio technician to makeover your voice, then you are in trouble. You want the sound technician to give your vocal quality optimum conditions. Later, if you or the producer decide to add other effects for mood or ambience, it's easier to do. Either way, the more resonance you bring to the microphone the better you'll sing. In addition, you won't become as tired during a taping or show.

Yet, we all have a natural microphone system! I call it our Magic Microphone, experienced primarily as vibrations in the front of the face. The spine and ribs also act as sound conductors—not only for the emerging sound, but also for better hearing. In fact, the whole skeleton vibrates with sound.

Whether we sing with a real microphone or not, we must train to open up our own natural microphone system. When you discover and fully experience that your body is actually *containing* waves of sound, you will realize that you don't have to push to get the sound out! This means, the muscles of your throat remain uninvolved, unless you use them for an effect.

Different styles of vocal resonance

For contemporary music, singers employ a brighter vocal tone, belting, mixed register tones and vocal effects utilizing microphone techniques. Opera singers, unlike pop or musical theater singers, need to train their bodies differently in order to support the extended legato lines they sing and to project over a 60 to 90-piece orchestra in a 2,000-seat theater, without a microphone. This kind of vocal power and projection isn't required for other singers.

Vocal resonance is not in the soft tissues of the throat. It is in the cavities in the front part of our head: the roof of the mouth, behind the upper teeth and the areas near the nose and cheekbones. In classical vocal training, this is referred to as "*The Mask*."

The Mask, is not only a natural "microphone" — it also contains our own special keyboard, where the notes are found. Lower notes are often felt in the mouth, at the teeth level, and even in the chest area. (Sing a low note and place your hand on your chest. You will feel the vibration.) The higher the note goes, the more it's felt above the upper teeth, all the way to the bridge of the nose and even the top of the head.

Remember, you are not a piano with a six-foot wide keyboard! All your notes are found in area of *The Mask*, a space spanning from your chin to the bridge of your nose and forehead that measures only five to six inches. The interior of the mouth's hard palate is shaped like an acoustical shell or dome as we often see on concert stages. We fill this space with our sound, fueled by a finely spun current of air.

Singers learn to develop awareness of the subtle vibrations and sensations felt in the frontal part of the face, and in this interior dome of the hard palate. This awareness grows with time and study, giving a singer consistency of tone and vowel color.

The greater your vocal resonance is, particularly in the middle voice, the better your vocal control becomes. Healthy resonance allows the breathing to flow more easily and adds power to the voice. The throat itself has no power to project sound, being of soft and non-vibrating tissue. It only houses the vocal cords. The chords must be free of extrinsic muscle tensions, in order to close properly and vibrate on the air pressure sent from the lungs.

The positions of each tone can be identified in the Magic Keyboard. In addition, this is where mixing of vowel resonances or tonal colors such as darkening or brightening of tones can be made. Regardless of the tonal colors chosen, achieving healthy resonance regulates the amount of breath pressure used, helping the vocal cords to vibrate with less effort and strain.

Two Exercises: Awareness of Resonance
Level 1: Buddha Smile with a Hum
(*The Buddha, Founder of Buddhism, is always portrayed sitting calmly with a little smile on his lips*).

- Sitting comfortably, without collapsing your chest, lean a bit forward in your chair.
- Drop your head just a bit, so there is no tension in the back of your neck.
- Now, feel just the corners of your lips curving *slightly* upwards, as in a Buddha Smile.
- Gently breathe naturally, for a few moments through the nose.

- Keep lips soft and full, in the Buddha smile.
- On a comfortable note, gently hum an "mm" and hold it for a beat or two. Repeat.
- Now, sustain it longer, and increase the feeling of the "mm" in your face. You may notice "mm" vibrating along the teeth, under the nose and in *The Dome* — the front of your face.
- Try it again. The "mm" of the hum felt in the front of the face may make your face or lips tingle, which is very good.
- Still humming, let the voice slide up and down some notes. Do this at moderate tempo.
- Combine with delicate *staccatos,* crisp little hums. Alternate between this and sliding of notes.
- Repeat. Be playful. It should feel good and easy to do.
- Place your hand on the back of the neck or on the area of the heart, to feel the Hum vibration.

When you do the Hum, it is important to keep your posture relaxed yet tall. Notice if your shoulders are tense or high up. Swing your arms gently, to relax the shoulders and ease up your breathing.

If you aren't feeling vibration in the front part of the face, try pressing gently along the sides of the nose and around the cheeks. Environmental pollution or allergies can affect the sinus areas, which can easily get clogged as well as cause excessive phlegm on the vocal cords. However, the hum should not be felt locking or pinching the sound solely in the nasal area.

Level 2: Buddha Smile with Sound

- Sit comfortably. Don't sag in the upper chest area. Move a bit forward over the hipbones and drop the head down a bit.
- Begin a resonant Hum at a medium pitch range. Hold the note for 4 beats, pause and repeat. Repeat this sequence three times.
- Now release the Hum to the sound *Wee* then, *Woe* (sounds like no). (The EE vowel energizes; the OH vowel relaxes; rounding out the resonation).
- Keep the mouth small! Let the sound last a few beats, even flowing downwards in pitch. Pause and repeat this *Wee* and *Woe*.
- Repeat this sequence three times.

(A small mouth position helps keep the jaw hinge in a more relaxed, neutral position. In Chapter 17, this will be covered in more depth.)

- Keeping the Buddha smile, start the Hum again.
- Now, from that place, sing a short phrase from one of your songs, keeping the mouth small. Notice how your voice feels in *the Mask*.

You can find of these kinds of warm-ups in my CD: *VOGA™ Warmups in 9 minutes or less!* (www.shurvoice.com). Not only are they extremely effective, they are also fun to do.

CHAPTER 7

Sound Waves, Vowels and Resonance

The scope of sound waves, vowels and resonance requires a live demonstration, rather than a book, but there are some important concepts we can touch upon in this chapter.

The science of sound is fascinating. The Hindu spiritual traditions have long ago mastered this science, along with the ancient knowledge of the power of mantra and sacred chant. One of the paths I've taken over the years has been the chanting of beautiful mantras. This daily practice has given me joy and profound insights into the nature of our vocal gifts.

Your voice is part of who you are. Your body contains the vibrations of your voice directed by your mind and heart. We must learn how to contain our sound. Sound travels outward in waves; propelled by its own energy and cannot be pushed forward by our efforts.

Each vowel has a certain frequency and shape. Therefore, the pitches or notes must pass through this shape as smoothly as possible. This is either preceded or followed by the consonants. While easy to write about, this vocal principle is not always easy to understand or put into practice. However, it is the foundation for establishing legato and tonal beauty.

Materializing the inner sound

Your voice is unique. It emerges from your body, mind and soul, animated by your musical intelligence. Throughout your life, you will continue to develop your instrument.

Learning about our voice is never boring. Think about it. You hear a melody, remember it, get an accurate mental impression of it, open your mouth and out it comes. What a wonderful, mysterious power that is.

Let's return to sound waves. Remember that in order for sound waves to travel easily, the waves must be contained somewhere. For sound to be heard well, some kind of acoustical, hard shape is required. When you see choirs performing on stage, they frequently stand in front of a hard portable shell. This kind of dome helps the sound to travel and be heard more easily. A sound system won't be heard clearly if it's covered up by a blanket, right? For singers this refers to the roof of our mouth — the hard palate. As mentioned in the previous chapter, this is called *The*

Mask, or *The Dome* — part of our natural microphone system that contains our sound.

To sing with ease and power, I encourage students to focus on sending a finely focused flow of air and tone, directly to *the Mask*. When you have good resonance there, it feels like very fine vibrations in the lips, around the upper teeth, nasal and cheek areas.

Our sound is contained not only in the bony chambers of our face, but also in the spine and ribs. These all act as sound conductors — not only for the outflowing sound, but also as sound conductors for your actual ear.

Making it appear effortless

Vocal greatness doesn't happen in a vacuum. Having total command of the stage takes a combination of natural talent, experience performing in a variety of venues, and regular vocal practice. Really good performers, even if they make mistakes, give the audience the impression that their art is effortless.

Your ability to remain focused — present to the music, the audience, the other people on stage, the conductor or the ensemble you are in — deepens each time you perform.

Whether you perform with a microphone or not, the better your vocal projection, the easier your singing and energy will flow. Putting less physical strain on the voice frees you to concentrate on the inner meaning of the lyrics and emotion you feel from the music. Your gestures and acting can then emerge with conviction and authenticity, along with helpful inspiration.

We are not carrying around a finished instrument with us all the time. That is why we need to allow time for daily study to master our voice. Whether you start with modest or abundant natural talent, if you are persistent, intelligent and willing to perfect your art, you can go far.

More about resonance

It only takes hearing a few notes or phrases for a top voice teacher or judge to rate a singer's level. As a vocal judge, my listening skills and kinesthetic intuitions are very sharp. In lessons, however, I evaluate holistically before making final judgements, considering a singer's overall talents and goals.

If you're holding and squeezing out vowels and notes from your body, while it may sound loud to you, it may not travel so well in the hall. Using a microphone will help, of course. However, over time, singing in this stressed way can compromise your voice. No matter whether you perform opera or popular music, ongoing issues with notes and vowels made with too much throat or breathing tension, stiffness of jaw muscles or the tongue should be resolved as much as possible. You want minimal tensions in there, since these interfere with resonance, energy flow and stamina.

Particular attention must be given to the muscles of the jaw hinge. If they are overly tense, it affects the smooth emission of vowels and consonants. Jaw tension also freezes up the breathing system. It gives you a locked up feeling. It also reduces resonance—that wonderful sensation of vibration in the bony parts of your face—affecting the clarity and beauty of vocal tone.

Vocal control is better achieved when you have found a good balance between optimum resonance and breath control. Without proper resonance, your voice remains pinched, flat, and lacks distinction. A free and "natural" sounding voice contains sufficient resonance, clarity and projection of tone with a pleasing, yet distinct, individual sound.

As mentioned in earlier chapters, singers need to hear a wide envelope of aural frequencies to keep their listening skills sharp. If you can't hear yourself well, you start to force your voice. Therefore, it helps to use the natural resonance of the room you sing in, as your built-in feedback system. The better the acoustics in the room or the concert hall, the easier it is to sing well.

I recommend adding practice sessions using a good room with decent acoustics in order to hear your voice better. That being said, it would be nice if every venue we sang in had great acoustics. In reality, this doesn't happen very often. Some spaces have very dry acoustics, others too much echo. When you practice, try to find a good spot in your home, where you can hear yourself better. However, we can't rely on any room or hall's acoustics to be our only feedback system!

Therefore, as we progress in our studies, we learn to "feel" our singing as much as hearing it. That's why that old rule pertaining to singing is a good one to remember: *"Don't listen to yourself so much."* Isn't this a paradoxical statement? When practicing, be aware of your sound, but also keep track of what it feels like; the physical sensations needed to achieve good singing. After a while, this kind of awareness becomes instinctive, making it easier to focus on expressing the music, rather than worrying about how you sound.

Recording yourself is another excellent study habit, as well as practicing by observing yourself in a mirror. These self-correcting habits can be very productive throughout your singing life.

However, singers can't hear or see themselves perfectly. Therefore, they need another pair of eyes and ears to give them honest feedback. Having trusted and respected voice teachers, conductors, and musical coaches is essential not only in a singer's preparatory studies, but throughout a career.

CHAPTER 8

You Never Can Tell!

Surprising Outcomes
How a Teen Girl's Efforts Paid Off

Just as a plant naturally develops when given proper care and set in the right direction, with proper guidance, and sufficient time, so will a singer's voice grow and blossom.

Initially the voice and talent may be rather modest. However, with intelligent application and willingness to learn, much can be achieved. Whether your talent is great or small, steady practice and continued vocal studies can develop your talent in surprising ways.

I often encounter talented teen girls who believe that after just one or two years of vocal study, they can begin a career. However, many teens' voices are still growing and may not become completely formed until their early or even late twenties.

Generally, entering a singing career before a student is ready can lead to losing one's confidence along with one's voice. We frequently see talented, young voice contestants sing their all in TV shows. Right afterwards they must face harsh criticism in full view of the public, smile, and carry on. This part is really hard to do. However, being a professional singer or even a dedicated amateur singer requires the ability to handle rejection and critical feedback — or, what may be even more difficult to handle, an indifference to one's performance.

However, when it comes to their voice lessons and taking constructive direction, suddenly the student knows better! So many voice students resist being corrected. They are impatient with the study of vocal method and just want to sing!

Part of a good teacher's art is finding that teachable moment, understanding when and how to guide the student in the right direction. Vocal study is a two way street. The voice teacher is always evaluating, and nurturing the unique sound, talent and potential of a student. During this process, the student requires sufficient time to understand what the teacher is imparting. Most importantly, a student requires patience since her voice, musicality and understanding may take some time to develop.

How a teen girl's efforts paid off

A lovely young singer, let's call her Nora, came to study with me after taking two years of lessons with my mother. A senior in high school, she was the alto section leader in her school's prestigious chamber choir, and an outstanding academic student. Although a good musician, able to learn her music well, Nora's actual voice was not particularly remarkable or memorable.

She had made steady progress studying the basics with my mother, but her vocal quality still had a kind of dullness to it, with an uneven and slow vibrato. With my mother's enthusiastic endorsement for a fresh approach, Nora began to study with me.

We had only about four to six months to work intensively before Nora went off to college. I asked her if she was willing to make some radical changes in her singing, and she agreed. We focused on addressing the core issues: intonation, vocal timbre, power, and resonance.

She came to lessons with enthusiasm and intelligence—two qualities essential to learning. I first gave her specific jaw and chin exercises to relax the muscles in that area. It was slow at first, but after about six weeks, we saw a definite change. The reconditioned muscles relaxed, staying in position with less tension. Nora was given specific breathing exercises that create a flexible and easy support. We then added rapid *vocalizes* and *arpeggios* (scale patterns covering an octave or more). Some of these were familiar to her from being in choir, but many were new to her.

These adjustments in her voice placement and breathing coordination helped to expand her voice. Instead of having just a limited alto range, she was able to sing into the higher soprano range for the first time. She was experiencing results and gained more trust in these new routines. At this point, we decided it was time to address the overall quality of the voice.

This meant making adjustments that were more radical. We moved out of the classical style of making *round tones* that she had been taught in choir. The idea she had about this round, classical style tone was correct, but it wasn't working for her. She was attempting to have this kind of classical sound, but did it imperfectly. Her tones were made too far back in the throat, causing a reduction in her overall resonance. This contributed to extra tensions in her jaw and flow of breath. Many choir directors want singers to make this *round tone* but don't have the proper time to spend on it during rehearsals. As a result, singers may not understand this correctly. Furthermore, choir directors can't replace the benefits of private vocal instruction.

I put Nora on a "vowel diet" for all *vocalizes*, scales and songs. We used what I call the bright *"pop music"* style of vocal sound. She tried some scales and phrases using a wider, smiling mouth, vocalizing with a very forward, exaggerated "Á" (sounds like the vowel in words like Fan, Can or Band). If you listen to great pop singers, they may use this kind of sound. And, just like great opera singers, great pop singers can be excellent vocal models!

On the first attempt singing a scale in this new position, the effect was immediate. Nora's voice woke up. Her facial expression brightened, her mouth went into a slight smile, and the jaw relaxed. She sounded fresher and more vibrant. The integration between middle voice and some of the higher range was improved, as were her lower notes.

I then suggested to Nora that she think of herself as a soprano, to help focus this "brighter" sound. (For some mezzo-sopranos and altos, it's helpful to maintain the higher overtones in the voice by thinking and listening to one's voice in this way.) Initially, singing in this new position made her feel strange, but she couldn't ignore the improvement that had resulted.

This kind of "vowel diet" is very effective for some of my other students as well. Putting certain voices in this radical "*can/band*" position, adjusts overly dark vocal placement, and other imperfect vocal placement issues. Paradoxically, I've found that using this approach (particularly for American singers), gives a more perfect classical vocal sound. It can give opera singers a more vibrant Italianate, "*forward*" placement, which for certain voices, or in specific repertoire, yields excellent results.

After a few weeks or more of this strict, bright "vowel diet" and having *all* her vowels move into this position, Nora's voice stabilized in this brighter sound. As her studies with me concluded, her tendency to go flat in ascending passages was gone and her vibrato had sped up. Nora was also noticeably less tired from the act of singing, and I saw her smiling more at each lesson! I congratulated her on making such a dramatic improvement and encouraged her to consider more voice studies in college.

By the time she left for college, Nora's voice had settled into this new vocal position and she was more confident about her singing. While she continued using a soprano timbre in her vocal placement, her voice category was still that of a mezzo-soprano. She was now on the right path, and it would be a matter of time and opportunity to see whether or not she would blossom into a professional singer.

About five years later, I was attending a worship service at a prestigious congregation who had brought in special guest singers that day. I was impressed when a beautiful young woman came to the podium and began singing a solo. She had a distinctive mezzo-soprano voice with a shimmering brilliance, beautiful vibrato and excellent diction. Her voice, musicality and feeling clearly made an impression on the congregation. I wondered with whom she had studied. After services, when I came closer to the podium, I recognized my former student, Nora! What a transformation from the high school student who had struggled so much with her voice.

She now has an established reputation as a fine singer, with steady work as a soloist. All her dedication, intelligence and efforts to perfect her singing had paid off.

CHAPTER 9

The Singing Body

Warm-ups for Ease and Power
A Music Teacher Sings Again

The concept of the Singing Body is one that has served me well as a performer and teacher. We sing with our entire body. We follow the sound of our voice as it emerges from us. Our posture and core strength is tall, strong, grounded and flexible. Our breathing system and kinesthetic controls must allow musical and vocal feeling to emerge. We sing through and with the body.

After the Singing Body is established, you can better manage inevitable performance jitters and consistently perform with your best sound. However, mastering the feeling of your Singing Body requires time and many performances in various venues, situations and audiences. The voice is never the same each night, but we can create optimum conditions for it.

We want our Singing Body to be flexible yet strong; responsive to the physical charge of our voice and emotions. We use our mind to participate with the Singing Body and the subtle sensations of vibration, resonance and articulations that occur when we sing. It doesn't matter what kind of music you perform. You can sing with or without a microphone, on the opera stage or in a recording studio. Either way, your instrument is rooted in your body, mind and spirit.

First, you must understand how important posture and body alignment is, and how this affects your sound as well as your state of mind! This requires patience to perfect, but is worth the effort, if we want to become better singers. As you develop a Singing Body, you may also develop a larger chest area, which gives the illusion of a slimmer waist...provided you avoid eating lots of potatoes and cakes, of course.

Breathing, Voice and Body Alignment

Since singing involves our breathing system, it is impacted by the condition of the central nervous system. The seat of the nervous system is located at the top of the diaphragmatic region, right below the mid-point of the top upper ribs. (For women, you find this mid-point at the upper ribs between the breasts.) If you are feeling emotionally upset, stressed, or tense, that nervous system area tightens automatically, reducing your energy and breath.

When your body, posture and vocal alignment are functioning well, you breathe more freely and even hear your own voice better. We also hear through bone conduction—part of the listening mechanism that regulates vocal quality and speech, which the great French audiologist, vocal therapist and educator, Alfred Tomatis discovered in his research. Therefore, the voice you produce can either positively charge your entire body and nervous system, or fatigue you.

That same central nervous system misfiring can also upset your performance or make singing feel physically painful. Therefore, we must learn how to train our singing body to **sustain and welcome** that powerful rush of adrenaline needed to perform. These kinds of performance energies can then become the fuel that **inspires,** rather than shuts down, your Singing Body. My system of warm-ups not only develops healthy vocal function but also reduces typical performance stress and anxiety.

Imagine this scene: you are in a busy, hectic cosmopolitan city and are stuck in traffic. You need to get to the theater for a performance or audition. You arrive stressed-out, tense and anxious. Now you need to get ready. You feel anxious and worried. You are tired today and your voice feels rather foggy. Nervous energy is taking over and making you feel even worse. Your throat feels tight and you're getting really freaked out. Somehow, you get through the audition or performance. But, at what cost?

To be a great singer is to feel things deeply. However, this ability for feeling things, which we prize in performance, can affect a singer's delicate nervous system in daily life. Singers need to feel things but not be overwhelmed by their emotional sensitivity. It isn't easy and we're not always able to control our sensitivities. And, unless you have a very laid-back personality, experiencing every day regular stress can impact your practicing and performing. We need effective vocal and physical methods that dissolve physical stress quickly and efficiently.

Some of these stresses, however, can be reduced with simple time management techniques. Make time for breaks from practicing, networking or other business demands. Take a walk. Plan your day carefully on the week and day of a concert or audition. Create clear boundaries about your availability for family or friends during those times in particular. Monitor how much you speak and sing before and after performances.

A period of silence and quiet is almost mandatory for most singers on the day before, and on the day of, a performance. However, some people just want to go about their normal routines on the days they perform, adding in an extra period of rest. Another excellent way to manage nervous energy is to take a good walk, or practice some hatha yoga on the morning of a performance.

Taking regular and weekly walks in a park or in nature is wonderful. Sitting still and breathing in a slow and deliberate way is also good. If you meditate regularly that is fantastic. Chanting sacred mantras is incredibly healing. Doing this before a performance is very beneficial.

When you can bring the experience of meditation and stillness into your performance, you begin to experience a profound shift in the quality of your breathing and mental state. Instead of trying to reach out to the audience, you experience a still inner focus that captures the audience's attention, drawing them nearer to you and the atmosphere and mood you set.

Why traditional *vocalizes*, are not enough

Rather than doing warm-ups with traditional vocal exercises using many scales and scale patterns (*vocalizes*), I like my students to start with targeted warm-ups for breath and posture, in order to release daily tensions and stresses. Singing is a kind of athletic art. Like athletes, we need gentle warm-ups to limber and stretch our instrument. These kinds of warm-ups are part of my VOGA™ *voiceyoga for peak performance* methods.

I start with a stable physical position; sitting comfortably, without collapsing the ribcage. Then, I ask the student to shift the upper body a bit forward of the hipbones and to observe how they are breathing—in that moment. I ask them to take a small breath of air in, and exhale slowly. Then, the student is guided to feel something important about that exhalation. I ask the student to notice how there's a slight movement inwards, a bit below the belly button as the exhalation begins and ends. (A tug inwards; felt in the center area of the transverse muscle of the lower abdomen.) These subtle movements are best understood by doing. Let's try some now.

Level 1: Exhalation for Ease and Power
- Sit in a chair. Keep the spine long; head and neck straight; shoulders open, but not tense.
- Lower your head down, a bit.
- Now exhale on an audible, long and slow "*FF*" or "*SH*."
- Wait a millisecond. Repeat "*FF* or "*SH*."

Did you notice how the inhalation rebounds in? After saying *FF* or *SH*, the incoming breath automatically returns, slightly expanding the floating ribs. It should feel pleasant to do, without any strain on the diaphragmatic region above the waist.

Level 2: Exhalation with Vowels
- **Sitting**, lean a bit forward. Upper body leans a bit in front of the hipbones.
- Gently say a long *Fee-ee-ee*. Pause.
- Now say a long *Foe*. (*Sounds like "No".*)
- Now, say a long *Wee* gliding into a long *Woe*.

Start a bit higher in pitch and descend down a few notes. Do you feel silly? That is good!
- **Now stand**. Repeat 3 times slowly, Fee – Foe followed by *Wee* – *Woe* in a descending vocal line. As you sing, slowly move the arms gracefully, just above the waist.

What did you notice? Do this playfully. It is easy to do. It should make you feel good. Each time you repeat this, do it more simply, using less force.

When the coordination between the exhalation and inhalation functions with greater ease, it allows the mind to become calm. In this calmer state, it is easier to observe the kinesthetic aspect of singing. Doing vocal warm-ups correctly should also help reduce stress or performance jitters.

Doing my synergistic VOGA™ routines, students become aware of how their individual vocal function really works, how <u>their</u> body actually breathes; how the air moves out and rebounds back in. They identify where they hold tensions in these areas. Common vocal terms that many students learn like *"support the tone" "breathe deeply," "use your body"* including how to add or decrease volume while singing, start to make sense in a tangible way.

A Music Teacher Can Sing Again

When I was on the music faculty at the Levinsky College of Education in Tel Aviv, Israel, I taught a class of vocal fundamentals using my VOGA™ methods to a class of female music students, all upper graduates who were getting their master's degrees. Some were music teachers, teaching in the elementary grades.

At the beginning of the school year, I asked students to share what they hoped to learn and achieve in my class. One of my students, let's call her Sarah, a tall and imposing woman, with a strong speaking voice, stood up. Sarah shared how she loved to sing, and was working as a music teacher. However, while she used to have a good alto voice, after six years of classroom teaching and smoking a pack a day, her voice was a mess. She doubted that the raspy and limited voice she had could really change. Yet, she also admitted she'd never studied voice before, so maybe, just maybe, she asked — would taking this class help fix some of these issues?

As I listened to her speak, I heard the passion she felt for singing and how much she wanted to regain her voice. In a flash of intuition (which sometimes happens to me when I teach), I responded and said, "Sarah, you may be surprised at what could happen. After working with some of the vocal methods that you're going to learn in this class, I think many things will change for you. And, I bet that by the end of this year, you may not even want, or need, to smoke anymore." She smiled, and her face lit up. She sat down and with a laugh said, she was ready to see what could happen.

After two months of classes learning my VOGA™ *voiceyoga for peak performance* and *Bel Canto* exercises, she began to feel significant changes. There was a reduction in muscle tensions and increased ease in her breathing. As the classes continued, her voice and singing improved noticeably. Her range expanded and the high notes she thought were lost were coming back in, clear and strong as well. She was a great student.

At the end of the first semester, she couldn't believe how well she was singing again. When it was time for winter break, Sarah stood up and proudly announced to the entire class some stunning news.

With a big smile, speaking in her now resonant and clear voice, this lovely teacher said, "I want you all to know, that after smoking a pack a day, for years, I've finally quit smoking! I never thought I could do it, but this class has really changed things for me. I am just so happy to have my voice back again, and to really sing."

She was radiant and confident. Being able to sing better than she had ever thought possible, had also affected her ability to breathe easily and deeply. The entire experience was so transformative and fulfilling, that she had all the ammunition needed to quit smoking. As the year progressed, she stayed off smoking and continued to improve in class.

As a teacher, it is very inspiring for me to facilitate and witness this kind of personal and vocal transformation. My students' experiences are precious, reminding me of the healing effect that music and singing can have in our lives.

CHAPTER 10

Words, Words, Words

Accessing your full vocal abilities requires mastering something that is unique to singers: words. No other instrument has words. This seems obvious, but we tend to forget this important distinction. Pianos certainly don't have words. They just have notes. Singing with open vowels or with one syllable is easy. Once you add the words to your song, vocal trouble begins. Words, made from an ever-changing series of vowels and consonants—are the cause of much of the difficulty for singing, no matter what the language.

In a live setting, having clear and crisp diction is an asset. It is also a must for projecting your voice into a concert hall. Using a microphone or vocal styling to blur or distort words should be a choice, not a sign of limitation. In performance, your musical expression and vocal tone can captivate us, but your diction shouldn't be forgotten in the process.

The words you sing are then projected from your mind, into the ears and minds of the listener. Isn't that a kind of magic? The words in a song affect the rhythm and phrasing. This is also called being musically intelligent.

You should practice how to shape and release consonants. How does each syllable of each word create a resonance? Learn how to sing the notes **through** the **shapes** of the consonants and vowels. The consonants create a frame for vowels. Together they make for dramatic expression. Articulating consonants elastically should cause a distinct yet subtle movement inwards, right below the belly button in the transverse abdominal muscles, improving breath support.

Opera singers are frequently at fault here. We get so preoccupied with the making of beautiful tones and vowels that we forget to spend equal time with consonants. Pop singers are sometimes even worse. The best diction today is often on the Broadway stage. Some singers feel they don't need any diction at all! I don't mind if it's a style or cool mood that a singer is creating, as long as when they do need strong and clear diction, they possess the technique to do it.

Why having good diction helps us sing better

Practice your words **separately** from your music. Take four to seven words at a time, first speaking them slowly. Then, break down each syllable phonetically. For example, the word "I" phonetically, is made up of a long *Ah* followed by a short *ee*. (See my *Recommended*

*Reading List; American Dictio*n). Each language has its own diction rules, which you must know. Then, adapt the diction to suit the vocal style of the song, as needed. In opera, balanced diction and vowels are preferred. In country or rock, diction can be less pointed, and more speech-like in some places. (This also occurs at times in opera.)

Breaking down each word by its consonants and phonetic components can be extremely productive. In my lessons, I teach students how to practice doing this in a precise way. Students learn how to elongate and intone each syllable in a systematic fashion. It also helps them in memorization of text. (In my *VOGA*™ *Warmups CD*, I demonstrate this.) After several days practicing your words only, the song should feel easier to sing. Doing this can be tedious and even boring, but the results are well worth the effort.

We must sing through the vowel shapes and consonants elastically, allowing the notes to flow accurately through these shapes. Every vowel and every consonant has its own frequency. Singers should fall in love with that. Therefore, the words must be mastered and made to flow easily from one to the other in the best positions possible. Vowels sung with minimal distortions attain their optimum frequency, allowing the voice to flow easily from note to note.

You should also practice the text or lyrics, as an actress would declaim her lines to find the emotions and gestures you will need when performing. Doing this kind of preparatory work for your songs or musical roles is essential. This brings extra depth to your art. Then, when you perform on stage or on a recording, the emotion in your heart comes through your voice and touches the heart of the audience.

As you learn about singing, continue to develop a fascination with words, vowels and consonants — shaping them, coloring them, spinning beautiful tones with them, and squeezing them or elongating them if needed for effect. Each language has its own issues and complexities. I speak fluently in two languages and decently in several more. I love the tonal qualities and feelings evoked by speaking or singing in different languages! Additionally, each language gives you a different persona as well.

Delivering the Message

Singers are born to express the feeling and message of music. It's our job. We are messengers and have something to say with our singing. Therefore, the music and songs we choose should mean something to us. Whether we sing other people's music or our own, we represent the composer and the poet. When we perform, our job is to *"deliver the message."* How the audience responds to the message, is not fully under our control. Our part is to focus on delivering it the best we can.

I believe that without clear projection of words and good diction, your performances can be limited.

Diction gives you more options for style, expression and of course, clarity of message! For example, the international musical theater star, Patti Lupone, not only has a magnificent voice but also superb diction, musical style and dramatic flair.

Along with detailed diction studies, remember to approach the text as if you were an actor on stage. This helps to going beyond being known as a singer with a beautiful or unique voice. Doing this may require extra creative homework, even when the meanings of the lyrics or text seem obvious.

When I ask my students questions such as *"What does this song really mean to you? What does this poetic phrase mean, what does it refer to?"* oftentimes, they are surprisingly clueless. If you don't understand the poetry, take the time to do so until you can understand it fully, and relate to it on a personal level. You don't need a degree in literature to become a singer, but it certainly helps to have basic understanding of poetic devices and metaphor.

Hearing and singing music is an emotional experience. As singers, if we don't connect personally with the music we sing, it shows. Once we do, our emotions can give new depth to our voice. When we have enough innate talent to match that understanding, our performances on stage or in recordings can touch the heart and soul of another person, a nation, or even an entire generation.

CHAPTER 11

Moving Parts: Vowels and Glides

Since the advent of microphones, we have become lazy in general with our overall diction. In the past, without amplification, actors and singers really had to "spit and spin out" words to be understood in a concert hall or from a stage.

As discussed in the previous chapter, consonants must be perfected! They must be made with speed, flexibility and energy. The consonant helps you to project the voice with ease. You can guide the vowel better if you release it with a fully supported consonant. The trick is to avoid over clenching the jaw or chin area. This is covered more in the chapters about tensions in articulation, jaw, tongue, lips, etc. The moving parts of the words (vowels and consonants, with their articulation system), must be mastered. The purer you can make your vowels, the better the overtones and resonance in your voice. Once you find the optimum position for your vowels, you can change them, bend or color them depending on the style of your music. For example, you could make the vowels brighter or darker, nasalized, or covered. Every voice needs a different amount of bright or dark sound. Having optimal balance in your tone doesn't take away from your unique sound—it liberates your singing mechanism.

Therefore, an important aspect of vocal training is establishing this optimum tonal balance in each singer's voice. In the traditional Italian *Bel Canto* terms, this means achieving a *Chiaroscuro* (*light-dark*) balance: an equalization of bass and treble frequencies in the voice. This balance creates an especially pleasing and vocally productive resonance. Having this kind of *Chiaroscuro* tonal quality is often associated with having an outstanding caliber of voice.

Vowel placement and breath control

Each vowel has a shape through which the notes or pitches pass. This also affects how much resonance you'll feel in the front of your face (the nasal passages, the teeth and the hard palate). Each syllable is also a sound wave of a particular frequency and range. The knowledge of how to release and sustain the phonetic components of syllables assists in healthy development of our vocal function and breathing mechanism.

We must make the vowels and consonants flow clearly and smoothly, avoiding abrupt changes in the throat or in our breathing. Once we master a smooth flow from syllable to syllable, we can add a *staccato* attack here and there, as needed to create crisp and clear articulation of the notes. We can modify the intensity of this attack and make deliberate choices about diction and tone as needed for each song. Certain words in a phrase can be emphasized for clarity of meaning. The entire phrase of the song must then be animated with your feeling and imagination.

The words of a song change the inherent lengths of the written notation of the rhythm of the song. For example, if we sing something like, "*I love you today and always,*" the song's rhythm will be affected by how we sing the word "I" (*long Ah + short ee*), and the other words. How you stress or elongate certain words and syllables is part of what a good voice teacher helps you to understand and perfect.

Connecting phrasing with vowels

We need to know some basic rules about any language in which we sing, particularly our own. For example, as mentioned previously, when singing the word "I" especially if the note is held for a few beats, you sing a longer "*AH*" and only at the last second of the note go to the "*ee*" part. This important aspect of the mechanics of diction applies to singing in any language.

Singing requires a different coordination than when speaking in conversation. Vowels and consonants are sustained for a much longer time than in regular speech. To get a feeling for this, I insist that my students practice their song by first learning the notes and rhythm perfectly (singing the melody with just one or two syllables). When the melody and rhythm are accurately learned, add the words.

Practice the words by sliding and gliding each syllable up and down slowly, yet with good tone, until all the words flow easily and feel connected to the breath. This approach has many benefits, facilitating memorization while at the same time coordinating the entire vocal system. Usage of this kind of systematic and deliberate way of practicing words can solve many vocal problems.

As you practice, try to glide words through the musical notes. This gliding action is part of a good singer's method and expressive art. Learning how to glide the voice properly is the basis for mastering the art of the *legato* and especially *portamento* (carrying of the voice smoothly, from note to note). *Portamento* not only makes singing easier in certain passages, but also is an essential expressive device. It is often indicated in the music by the composer, and is heard in both classical and non-classical vocal music. Whenever *portamento* is used, it must be placed at the appropriate moment in the phrase, with elegance and good musical timing.

CHAPTER 12

Keep Your Vocal Capital

When I was a young opera student in college, my voice was very strong and healthy. I loved to sing and learn new repertoire, happily spending two hours every day practicing. This was easy for me to do. I was young and my voice was very fresh. I soon discovered, however, that in order to have the stamina needed to sing opera roles, less is sometimes more. Not every phrase has to be loud and strong.

As a graduate music student at Indiana University School of Music in Bloomington, Indiana, I became a voice student of the celebrated diva, the Romanian soprano, Madame Virginia Zeani. While close to sixty when she began teaching, her voice was still lustrous, brilliant and flexible. She could demonstrate anything and taught us what it means to sing opera with intelligence, passion and taste. She astonished listeners with her amazing coloratura and stunning low notes.

In addition to Virginia Zeani's stellar career, performing with other celebrated singers and many of Italy's greatest conductors, she had also studied opera with Aureliano Pertile, the legendary Italian tenor who trained her amazing voice in the authentic *Bel Canto* traditions.

Don't leave your voice in the practice room!

Zeani insisted that I practice using what is called the *Half Voice*, or *Marking* technique, to conserve my vocal capital. She also showed me how to pace myself in operatic roles so that I didn't burn out by the last act. The great American soprano, Leontyne Price, was also known for championing this idea. She was often quoted on her delightful motto that when performing, you should *"sing on the interest and save the principal."* Since I usually sang full out in those days, for me this was a new idea!

While there are some very famous singers who always sing full out—even in rehearsals—they are the exception. It took me some time to master this approach, but now it seems natural to me.

If you're a talented teenager or a young woman in your early 20's embarking on a career, don't ruin your potential and burn out your beautiful voice by over singing or over practicing. This advice is not always easy to follow. It's a great experience to sing with all you've got. Many vocal competitions on television seem to demand full out singing. However, contestants must monitor themselves in order to keep their voice fresh for the next round in the show. In general, to do well in this field, singers must develop ways to handle pressure coming from managers or producers who ask them to sing music that just doesn't fit their voice or to perform when sick, hoarse or simply exhausted.

We must always strive to achieve excellence in our vocal *quality* rather than quantity or loudness per se. When you sing pop, musical theater, jazz, or opera, the more you develop a beautifully balanced and resonant sound, the less force you will need to project your sound. Your physical stamina will improve and your voice should hold up much better in the long run.

For my beginning and intermediate students, I encourage shorter practice periods, such as 10 to 20 minutes a day for warmups and *vocalizes*, followed by 10 to 40 minutes for repertoire. Practicing for 60 minutes a day for both technique and songs is fine, and will yield good results. The advanced singer could do 90 minutes a day of singing. If you want to practice beyond that (or beyond what your teacher recommends) or simply want to do more, then listen to your music, go over memorization or other preparation that doesn't require a lot of singing.

In my private studio, I also remind students to come well rested, hydrated and to have eaten before lessons. Singers expend a lot of energy when performing and studying. Students are shown how to practice efficiently, so that they can move past technique to artistry, finding subtexts for their songs, optimal phrasing, diction and emotion.

Once your musical skills and basic vocal technique are well established, performance skills must be added. There is so much more to do other than sing. It doesn't matter if you sing folk songs, pop songs, musical theater, or opera; you always have music to learn. You must not only fully memorize your own part, but also the orchestra or band accompaniment and any other ensemble parts in which you are included.

Singers must develop and work on acting skills. Some singers are extraordinary actors. However, not all gifted singers are equally gifted as actors. You should at least know how to move gracefully on stage and make the appropriate dramatic gestures as needed. Different acting skills are used for different musical genres. Musical theater and opera demand not only outstanding musical skills but also excellent acting ability. A more relaxed and subtle style of acting is seen for jazz and another for cabaret style shows, etc.

The classical vocal methods that I was fortunate to learn with Madame Virginia Zeani have kept my voice supple and flexible all these years. Nonetheless, I know what it means to lose one's voice, and not be able to sing due to injury or illness. As mentioned previously, during my early opera career in Europe that is what temporarily happened to me.

I had been performing at the Zurich Opera, Switzerland, without having fully recovered from a bad flu, which led to an inflammation of the vocal cords. Fortunately, I was referred by the opera house to a respected ear, nose, throat specialist in Zurich, a Dr. Padovani. I immediately contacted him to begin treatments. Fortunately, I had two months off before my next opera engagements resumed.

Dr. Padovani's treatments included special vocal therapy methods that he had studied with a disciple of Frederick Alexander, founder of the *Alexander Technique*. (A mind/body discipline which assists in optimum flow of posture, movement and breath.) As I practiced these protocols and continued under Dr. Padovani's specialized care, I regained my voice in two months, singing even better than before, and just in time to return to the Zurich Opera house. I continued seeing him that year, to solidify my new practice. These protocols became an indispensable addition to my *Bel Canto* training.

While I was lucky to find the expert help I needed, the experience of temporarily losing my voice, the source of my livelihood, was terrifying. I realized that my understanding about myself and singing had to expand. This led me to making further studies about vocal function and alternate healing methods, including visiting India, learning meditation and the chanting of sacred mantras. These beautiful spiritual practices, which I continue to this day, have enriched my life, giving me a deeper understanding about how music and singing can heal and transform.

CHAPTER 13

The Sweet Power of High Notes

When I discovered my high notes at the age of 14, singing my first full voiced high G, two octaves above middle C, I nearly fainted. The sensation definitely made me feel light headed, but also intrigued. Taking a breath to recover, I sang the high note again. This time I focused on the quality of the note, and it sounded *powerful!* The resonance and vibrations I felt in my head were amazing. I couldn't wait to learn some more classical songs, especially those with exciting high notes in them.

When I teach young teens or beginners, I remember these experiences. Many students report similar initial reactions singing above the staff, sometimes even feeling momentarily faint or dizzy from the experience. Fortunately, this soon passes, as students get comfortable with these sensations. At first, these high notes may sound soft or weak, but with continued practice, they do get fuller.

Before we speak further about women's high notes, we will compare our sound with men's voice types. The most common male voice is the baritone or lyric baritone. The deep bass voices and high tenor voices are rarer. The operatic tenor is the most difficult voice to master. Despite these categories, most men can also sing very high, switching into a distinctive sound that resembles a woman's voice, by using their *falsetto* voice, which in today's popular music is done quite often.

Conversely, in popular music, songs for women are generally performed in the lower range of the female voice due to a preference for a more relaxed sound. It's also harder to understand lyrics when they are sung on much higher notes. This means that many female pop singers rarely sing out of the middle or low range. Since the most common voice type for women is the soprano voice, this is the equivalent of asking a violinist to sound like a cello all the time. You can try, but it won't really work in the long run. The main thing to remember is that singing too low or too high all the time is fatiguing for the vocal cords.

Redefining our feminine side

I believe that we need to reevaluate our feminine mystique and reclaim it. The memorable women singers of past eras were expected to maintain and develop the sweetness and purity of their voice and to cultivate feminine charm, elegance, poise and grace.

Today it's a different era. We are frequently presented with movies, images and stories of strong and bold women doing what they want. The modern woman is expected to be assertive, independent and decisive. That is fine and well. However, what doesn't change is the fact that females certainly have different voices than men. Acknowledging that gender can affect our chemistry and behavior doesn't have to be a negative thing.

Being authentic as a singer means you can sing from the heart and the reality of your being. When you allow the feminine, vulnerable and sassy side to shine, it is Okay! Let your heart be soft, but keep your spine strong. When you allow the sweetness and gentleness of your feminine side to emerge in your singing, you may encounter some surprises, personally and musically. This could mean adding new repertoire or songs that use more of your full emotional and vocal range.

Female artists in pop or rock music are seldom valued for the sweetness and purity of their voice, no matter if they are sopranos or altos. The essential higher part of a woman's voice, that brings clarity and focus to the voice is simply misunderstood by students without a background or training in classical music. These students' ideas of what makes for good singing are heavily influenced either by hearing the soft and breathy female voices singing top 40 latest hits, or female artists with strong alto belting voices. Generally, rather than seeking clarity and beauty of tone and a voice that carries well into a hall, a wobbly, breathy and unsupported tone is preferred by young pop singers, in an effort to create an intimate, sexy sound. That is fine for making a vocal effect in a phrase. However, constantly singing with a wobbly or overly breathy tone quality, can cause breaks in the voice and vocal problems later on.

The importance of the *Head Voice*

The *Head Voice* proper begins at the middle register of the female voice. It should not be confused with a man's *"falsetto"* voice. It is usually felt as soon as you ascend the scale, shifting from chest sound into a lighter sound a few notes above middle C, to around F or G. For most voices, these notes already feel different since they employ a lighter vocal mechanism. When the shift occurs at A or B, above middle C, especially for untrained female voices, this may need to be re-set a few notes lower. The *Head Voice* proper, which employs more *head voice*, begins in the female singer's upper register around E, F, or G about an octave and three notes above middle C.

The higher part of the middle voice, up to the beginning of the *Head Voice* proper, should be exercised. Singers should practice making a smooth transition from the low voice to the head voice. Doing so keeps the voice supple and youthful. Having good high notes helps your low notes become even better.

Often, female teens seem to resist this higher voice. During my twenty years of teaching, I've encountered many untrained female singers, particularly those who sing popular music, who have never discovered how to sing in the higher part of their voice. When they do try singing higher, these notes sound weak or small in comparison to their low, more familiar sound. At first, this may be true, but usually within a year of training, these higher notes noticeably gain in strength.

Many students may even feel anxious or extremely uncomfortable just when singing in the middle register of the voice, for example only six notes above middle C, and are only happy if they can belt their way up from low G up to C above middle C. Yet most of them are unable to do this consistently, since the vocal mechanism cannot comfortably belt that high.

In popular TV voice shows and voice competitions, young girls barely out of their teens performing with a heavily produced sound, are admired. However, when singers with natural belting ability perform without knowing how to lighten up their sound at times, this can put too much pressure on their vocal cords, making it difficult to sing this way in the long run.

The quality of the *head voice*, which is a lighter vocal mechanism, can be extended throughout the range. This goes back to Chapter 12, *Your Vocal Capital*. You can use this function of the voice to "brighten" the middle and even the low notes. Conversely, the more muscular chest voice or the belting of lower notes adds strength and power to the high notes!

Once this integration of vocal registers is achieved, a singer's vocal range will naturally expand. In my teaching practice, I gently guide young singers to experience how to slide or glide into what I call "second gear" into the *head voice*. Keeping the upper part of your voice healthy and flexible ensures your vocal longevity. Additionally, having a bigger range, gives you more choices in the kinds of music you can sing.

While all female singers benefit from exploring the higher notes in their voice, opera singers have no other choice. They must have usable high notes. That being said, the middle and high notes for opera singers can also suffer from being made with too much chest sound or not enough chest voice. I like to remind my opera students not to overly darken their vowels, or place the sound too far back in the throat. They should not use too much of a muscular lifting of the soft palate or pressing down on the laryngeal area. The soft palate rises on its own and the larynx will stay in a neutral position when using the "hint of a yawn" approach, mentioned in previous chapters.

Many ambitious singers in classical music and contemporary music may start out in a career having exciting voices. If they are good performers as well, managers or conductors jump in with exciting offers to perform in shows and recordings, which is fine when the music chosen, fits the singer's voice and talent.

This brings us to the subject of saying *no* to requests by managers or conductors to sing particular roles or songs that don't suit your voice. Saying *no* means being willing to embrace our vocal limitations in a positive way. We need to make smart choices about what we can sing, or cannot sing. If you have a rich alto or soprano voice, and naturally sing with a heavy dramatic quality, chose songs or roles that emphasize those qualities. If you are a high lyric coloratura, it's best to sing roles or songs that emphasize the flexibility of your voice and your easy high notes.

It's actually empowering to identify vocal limitations. Not only for repertoire selections, but also in general, if you want to succeed as a singer. You may need to find the courage to say *no* when offered performances in music that is too light, or overly dramatic for your voice.

When you are a working singer, you should carefully review the whole work, the size of the orchestra or the type of ensemble with which you will sing, and try it out in sections. By doing this, you can usually assess whether you can do it comfortably or not. When you are at this stage in your career, you are probably confident enough to trust your judgement and instincts. You are prepared to take the responsibility for your choices. When you are unsure, don't hesitate to get good advice and feedback from your voice teacher, musical coach or trusted conductor. They know your voice, talents and strengths. While it is wise to get a second opinion about new roles or repertoire that you are considering, sometimes you must, and should, make these decisions on your own.

CHAPTER 14

Why Opera?

Fans of TV shows such as *The Voice* or *American Idol* prove that we value people with vocal talent. I'm all for TV shows that promote young singers. What concerns me is the tremendous hype that each singer faces, both in terms of the critique they receive and the inflated compliments and promises made.

The judges on these programs rarely discuss what it takes to stay in vocal shape. Attention is given to the singer's attitude, their "look," or lack of it, along with the hard work required, but never showing what that hard work actually is! Do we ever see them practicing scales, *vocalizes*, or learning how to do a phrase from a technical point of view? At most, you may see a scene where the singer is asked to sing with more "attitude" or told to "focus" or "relax."

To be competitive in commercial vocal music, adding some classical vocal technique is very helpful. You don't need to smooth out all your idiosyncratic style or sound, however, classical voice methods gives added vocal control and deepens one's musical skills.

Why I switched from musical theater to opera

When I was 16, I moved from Seattle, Washington where I'd been living with my dad, back to Los Angeles to live with my mother. By that time, I was a very good violinist and practicing diligently. I had also taught myself to play guitar and learned British and American folk ballads along with several classical art songs.

Living with my mom, I began taking voice lessons every week with her. At that time, my mother was not performing as much, but was running her very active private voice studio. She had many Hollywood actors and professional singers at her studio. Considered one of the best voice coaches at that time, she was sought out for her expertise as a voice teacher and piano skills. My mother taught me simple vocal scales and diction for opera languages. She also developed my repertoire, teaching me arias, art songs, musical theater and operetta. While I enjoyed doing this, I was still focused on being a classical violinist and played in some high-ranking student orchestras.

Maintaining my playing as a decent, if not spectacular, violinist required at least three and half hours of daily practice, and more on weekends. This was driving me crazy. And the few solo performances I had at the time were nerve wracking. I missed the ease of singing and being on stage, which for me, was a breeze compared to performing on the violin. But, I wasn't yet ready to give up the violin, especially after the four years of serious training I'd put in. As a compromise, I decided to continue studying both voice and violin, but reduced the intensity of my violin studies.

Studying with my mother, being in the high school musicals and in the elite choral ensemble helped me develop rapidly as a singer. Therefore, my mother encouraged me to enter a few local opera competitions, some of which I won. While I enjoyed singing classical music, my secret dream was to become a famous pop or musical theater performer.

Having grown up in a family of professional musicians, I knew that a music career required confidence and ease on one's instrument, since nerves can wreck the best of performances. Performing as a violinist made me far too nervous. It was just too stressful. So, after graduating from high school, I finally made the decision to give up violin. I realized that my real strength was in acting and singing on stage.

I attended the California State University, Northridge (CSUN), which at the time, had a very good opera department run by the highly respected Dr. David Scott. As an undergraduate, I was accepted into the opera performance track. Outside of classes however, I continued singing pop and musical theater. I wanted to touch a larger audience and have a more personal way with music, which these styles seemed to offer in abundance.

While exploring those options, I was engaged in opera chorus work with local Los Angeles opera companies and performed major soprano roles at the CSUN Opera Theater. Participating at the music program at CSUN finally convinced me that I really did have what it takes for an opera career. It seemed like a hard path to follow. Yet, I couldn't deny the fact that I preferred singing classical music and being in operas to other kinds of music. With the urging of my voice teachers and student colleagues, I dropped my other musical activities to focus exclusively on opera.

As a teacher, I like to remember these experiences; because it makes me more sensitive to the soul searching and musical exploration young singers often go through. Nonetheless, I remind students of a simple truth: whatever music you choose to sing—pop, jazz, opera or rock—if you are moved by it and it fits your voice, the audience will respond to your conviction. Therefore, find what you really love to sing and perfect it.

A judicious use of vocal techniques (belting, legit, speech-style, classical) allows a singer greater range and expressiveness in performance. When you sing a song, consider how much you base your technique merely on a vocal styling effect or quirky vocal mannerism. Solely imitating the musical style that is in vogue, whether it's classical or popular music, can get you off track.

Although classical music singers are expected to conform to precise vocal and musical standards, the training of professional contemporary and musical theater singers has its own set of complex demands and usually requires dance training as well. Therefore, when teaching pop or musical theater singers, I give them just enough of classical voice methods to help them succeed in their style.

Opera singers must study the hardest for their careers. They put in years of training to be where they are. Singing classical music in general, requires a quality voice, excellent musical and memorization skills and the ability to sing in several languages. Opera singers must also develop strong physical stamina to act and sing for hours on stage, often in heavy costumes.

Practicing *Bel Canto vocalizes*, however, must be done under the guidance of an experienced voice teacher, as these can be very taxing on the voice. They are like vocal gymnastics, and must be carefully studied for many years to perfect. Along those lines, I've prepared another Free Bonus for readers who want recommendations about some excellent *Bel Canto Vocalize Books*, with my comments about how to use them. Some of these books include song-like exercises showing how to sing Italian and English correctly.

FREE BONUS #3:
www.shurvoice.com/Bel-Canto-Vocalizes

CHAPTER 15

Your Money Notes

Those singers, who are known for having spectacular high or low notes, accurately singing fast scale passages (*coloratura*), or sustaining powerful final notes in a song, are what opera singers like to describe as "having the Money Notes." They can do this consistently well in performances, and have mastered the quality and volume of these special musical phrases, controlling them with apparent ease. People pay to hear and experience these thrilling moments.

Having these kinds of Money Notes in your voice is sometimes just part of your natural talent. For most of us, finding and keeping these notes, is a matter of practice, musical intelligence and skill. While reading about Money Notes can't replace a live demonstration, some aspects of this important subject will be covered in this chapter.

Let's further define what we mean by Money Notes in terms of where they are in a musical scale. For sopranos and tenors, it usually refers to your high notes, from high G, A, B and High C (two octaves above middle C for sopranos, and one octave above middle C for tenors). Impressive low notes would be low A, G, F and sometimes E below middle C. For mezzo-sopranos and altos, it can be both low and high notes. This is the same for basses and baritones. In opera, we glorify the quality of a tenor or soprano's wonderful high B or high C and for coloratura sopranos, their high D or E or even F (two octaves above middle C).

For pop music, Money Notes usually refer to any higher notes heard in a song. For country-western music, the juicy low notes are often the ones that count. Money Notes can occur in the middle or ending of a song, and are usually sustained for a few extra beats or more. These are the moments that we say, "give you the big bucks" when you sing, or when the judges on the TV show like *The Voice,* turn around and ring the bell.

Having memorable Money Notes is not reserved for highly talented singers. There is a method for them. The specific how and why is a little different for every female singer, and changes with the kind of song or aria that is being performed.

A general rule is to make a good connection on the notes before and after the Money Note. The actual high note can be sung either with a staccato release onto the note, or with a quick gliding from the lower note to the top note in the phrase. The amount and timing of this kind of slide between the notes must be practiced to achieve the best effect. This is referred to in classical vocal singing as using *portamento* (mentioned in previous chapters). It must be done elegantly and with good vibrato.

However, I suggest that you consider your entire voice to be full of Money Notes rather than any one note in particular. This takes the pressure off of your singing and performance in general. Anyway, you don't want to be just a one-note singer with only a few high or low Money Notes—do you?

Achieving secure high notes also means preparing what comes before and after those notes. Linger more on the preceding note, giving it good support and resonance. It's absolutely essential to plan how to sing these preceding notes and where you will breathe in the previous phrases. If you are not absolutely clear about where and how you breathe in the preceding phrases, you won't have a consistent strategy for the high notes. Practice the phrase exactly the same way each time, so it becomes completely automatic.

Sometimes that special note may be best accomplished with just a quick catch breath, more of a release done with a *staccato* attack *(a short attack on the note)*. Usually, to sing a high note, you should release the vowel or consonant of the word without force, avoiding any clamping down in your throat or jaw.

Keep the jaw area relaxed, yet without opening the jaw too far downwards either.

In addition, carefully analyze the phrase musically. Sing the phrase very slowly with additional focus on the elastic support and articulation needed for those notes. Then, work only with the words, breaking them down into syllables and make them fluent and elastic. If you are clear about what you are doing before, during and after the Money Note(s), it will make singing those phrases consistently better.

Typically, for high notes, the transition from middle to high voice may also be part of the problem. This is referred to in classical vocal training as the *passaggio* (Italian for passageway), the narrowing in the vocal cords between vocal registers. Sometimes this natural shift is out of balance and needs to be reset (see Chapter 13). Each voice has this narrowing, felt as a shifting in timbre and vocal quality around a few specific notes. Understanding how to manage this shifting in the *passaggio* is a key component to having easy high notes, and vocal training in general. It's what I call learning to *"glide or slide the voice into another gear"* to describe the sensation felt in this change of register.

Let's review a basic concept brought up in Chapter 4, *Sopranos Slide, Piano Keys Hit*. When you look at the piano keyboard, the "high note" appears way up there about 12 inches or more from middle C....wow. Such a long way to go up or down that keyboard! Immediately your eyes take over, shutting down your kinesthetic mind. Relying on your eyes sends an *up/down* message to the singing body. This makes your shoulders rise as you breathe in, and the larynx to go up, closing the throat in an uncomfortable manner. In this state, you can rarely sing music consistently well. It's helpful to eliminate the entire idea of going "*up and down*" when you sing, anyway.

However, in our body we have our own portable keyboard. Do you remember where that is? In *The Mask*. To review: the higher notes are felt as ascending vibrations behind the upper teeth or near the cheeks (closer to the bridge of the nose); the lower notes vibrate more in the mouth and teeth. The entire *Mask* area is only about five inches, from your chin to forehead, compared to the twelve to twenty-four inches between high and low notes on a keyboard.

You can easily feel how notes and resonance shifts in the *Mask*, when you hum or sigh out a phrase. However, the core body action for breathing (the power that releases the notes), shouldn't go up or down at all. Therefore, if your shoulders are rising every time you breathe or if you are gasping a bit when you breathe, this needs to be corrected. The actions of the larynx, the flexibility of the lower ribs and lower body breath support, must remain in equilibrium. To understand this requires both repeated practice, and fluency in singing through words. Good high notes, therefore, should be released without a tightening felt in the throat or a stiffening of the breathing reflexes.

I like to call the core actions of the breathing system the engine or motor of the voice. Breathing should not be identified with an idea of "*up and down.*" I like to replace this mental command with "*down and out.*" This feels as if slowly sighing down over the note. Conversely, for quality high notes, depending on the phrase, using a crisp release on a consonant may be effective. I often encourage students to add small arm or body movements for a difficult phrase, to free up the Singing Body and wake up the kinesthetic mind.

Exercise of Awareness:
Level 1: Easy Voice Release

- Sit comfortably yet alert in a chair. Your chin and neck are relaxed, not jutting out.
- Assume the Buddha Smile. Keep the mouth closed in this little smile.
- Inhale a tiny puff of air. Hold a millisecond.
- Open your mouth a bit, as you exhale on 4 beats.
- Repeat above sequence slowly, three times.
- Now, gently sigh out a long and easy *Mo*, or *Bo*, then just *Oh* followed by *No*. Repeat three times.

Did you notice how little air you needed to emit those tones?

- Now, sing a part of a song in the same way you sighed out *Mo* or *Bo*. What do you notice?

As we develop awareness of these subtle sensations, it changes our singing. Over time, we begin to experience our singing as a containment of sound and vibrations, rather than a pushing out of sound. Singing in this way feels great.

Another way to connect high and low notes smoothly is the traditional method of practicing the phrase in lower keys, followed by moving the phrase up in half-step increments towards the actual key. In other words, turn a difficult phrase into a fun vocal exercise. This method is often utilized in choirs.

Try practicing difficult phrases using any of these suggestions and relax your mind about it. After a few days, notice how it feels to sing those same phrases. Sometimes it may take several weeks to experience a positive change. Don't despair. Remember—you are not a piano with all the keys and strings perfectly in order. Give yourself some time to coordinate everything.

Eventually, things should stabilize. If not, the easiest fix of course, is to change the key of the song! Move the key either up or down as needed for your voice. For an opera role, naturally that won't be possible, unless you are a big star in the operatic firmament, although in other genres it can be done.

When I coach singers in pop, rock and jazz, we define where their optimum range is. Once determined, we can adjust the key of the song accordingly. I am often amazed how many times some singers in the music industry forget to make this perfectly acceptable adjustment to their songs.

CHAPTER 16

When Pop Meets *Bel Canto*

Healthy Vocal Function
How a Pop Singer Got Her Voice Back

Having appeared as a soloist in various operas and concerts as well as performing both soprano and mezzo-soprano roles, not only do I have a very large repertoire, but I understand the problems and pitfalls of both voice types.

Maintaining good vocal function is the cornerstone for a healthy singing and speaking voice. Though vocal function can be established, standardized and optimized, no two singers sound alike. Everyone has his or her unique sound signature. How wonderful! However, I address vocal function in most lessons, as this must be established before we can speak of vocal style. Let's remember a basic fact about our instrument. Singing takes up a lot of energy and breath control.

In this respect, the physical demands of singing are similar to playing a wind instrument such as a trombone, trumpet, or flute. This means that singing for extended periods of time can really be fatiguing; for advanced students, practicing two hours a day is usually enough.

However, since we are depending on our body and mind to sing, let's not forget a simple fact: it's imperative that singers rest and eat before a performance, practice session or a voice lesson. Make time for rest before and after vocal sessions, or learning a new role. Include taking a relaxing walk, stretching, or taking a nap on days you are training. Before you sing, drink some healthy liquids, tea or water. Vocal cords get dried out very quickly, requiring regular hydration.

In addition to taking care of your health and body, you must understand intellectually and kinesthetically how your own voice functions. This includes resolving or managing health issues such as upper respiratory conditions or allergies that can affect your singing. Our work is both athletic and mental, so we need to keep our daily habits simple, healthful and balanced.

Effective Practice Habits

Training of the voice for singing or speaking is a personal and transformative experience. To be successful in this endeavor, a student requires regular, weekly lessons and a willingness to change repertoire or musical styling when her voice requires it.

In times past, many serious voice students would go almost every day to their teacher for lessons in order to be carefully monitored and guided in all aspects of their practicing. Naturally, this was before we had video cameras, portable recording devices, or having to deal with driving in busy city traffic.

It takes a while for a student to understand how to practice effectively. In addition, when there are ongoing vocal problems, it takes effort and courage to re-train or resolve them, especially after any kind of surgery. It is unrealistic to expect significant vocal transformation to occur without the combination of enough time, expert coaching and daily practice. While some students may experience dramatic changes in a few months of study, most should plan on at least two years of regular weekly lessons, and three or more years to sing at an advanced level.

How a pop singer got her voice back

On a visit to see family in New York City, I met a lovely woman, whom we'll call Linda. With her naturally beautiful voice and stunning good looks, she had begun her career early as a brilliant teen singer. Now in her late thirties (still looking as youthful and beautiful as ever), her career was not as strong, but she was busy with various recording projects. She shared that she was seriously worried about her voice. Somehow, she couldn't sing as well as before and didn't know whether it was technique or a physical issue. We spoke about what this could mean and tried out a few ideas on the spot. She liked my approach and expertise. Promising to stay in touch, I returned to Los Angeles.

A short time later, Linda called me from New York City. She shared that she had discovered a physical cause for her vocal problems. This condition required surgery on her vocal cords. She asked me for recommendations about doctors. I recommended that she consult with Dr. Steven Marc Zeitels. Dr. Zeitels is responsible for the continued career of many top opera, rock, musical theater and pop singers, the most famous of his recent patients being the amazing golden-voiced Adele. Dr. Zeitels is the *Eugene B. Casey* Professor of Laryngeal Surgery at the Harvard Medical School and the Director of the Massachusetts General Hospital Center for Laryngeal Surgery and Voice Rehabilitation (*MGH Voice Center*).

I was personally aware of this remarkable voice surgeon with his unique laser inventions, before he received international acclaim from Adele's case, since my brother Michael, who is both an international airline pilot and an opera singer, had been a patient of Dr. Zeitels. The medical treatment that Dr. Zeitels gave my brother saved his voice. Encouraged by my personal recommendation, Linda decided to have her surgery done by Dr. Zeitels.

The surgery was a success. After the necessary post-operation recovery period, Linda contacted me again, to ask if I would help re-condition her voice and teach her more about vocal technique.

While blessed with a beautiful voice and natural singing talent, she had never taken real voice lessons, let alone done vocal exercises like five note scales, octave *arpeggios*, or rapid extended scales (*coloratura*). Since I was in Los Angeles, and she was in New York City, we decided to try Skype sessions.

The Skype sessions worked for us. Linda was a wonderful student: focused, analytical and hard working. She initially took voice lessons on a bi-weekly basis. After about eight weeks of these intensive sessions focused on reconditioning the voice with special vocal therapy exercises (to ensure smooth phonation, closure of the vocal cords, resonance, and breath pressure) and singing simple *vocalizes,* Linda's voice was noticeably improved. Significantly, she was experiencing less tension in her throat and breathing system while singing.

About three months into our Skype sessions, I felt she could do more advanced *vocalizes* to develop more endurance, resonance and range. For her voice, belting was out of the question, so this meant some *Bel Canto vocalizes* and traditions. Linda was very intrigued with these exercises and took to learning them with astonishing ease. About four months later, Linda was back in the recording studio. Her producer was amazed at the positive difference in her singing. The recording sessions were shorter and more productive than ever before, saving them both time and money.

In the weeks that followed, we added new repertoire to match the new voice. Linda now had easier higher notes, and could sing many of the beautiful Musical Theater songs she had always loved along with soulful Latin music. While her higher notes had blossomed and gained in power, her middle and low notes were also fuller, more resonant and secure than before. She now had a usable range of two octaves compared to her earlier range, which was only about one and half octaves.

Linda was also impressed by how my holistic approach to vocal work affected her overall energy. During the day, her speaking voice became more resonant and fluid. Even her posture, including her head and neck balance improved. Many of her previous breathing tensions had significantly reduced, giving her better physical stamina and mental clarity. Encouraged by these changes, she began to expand and revise her musical career options, energized with a new confidence in herself as a woman, artist and singer.

About a year and a half later, Linda ventured successfully into several new projects, singing better than ever. In collaboration with other musicians, she took on creating and producing original music that she believed in, as well as contributing her musical talents in support of various philanthropic projects around the globe. Her new recordings and concerts feature her beautiful voice in mystical chants with pop styling.

CHAPTER 17

What Can I do About My Tense Jaw?

Tensions in the muscles of the jaw and problems with the jaw hinge can become a chronic condition. When not corrected or dealt with, these muscle tensions have a negative effect on your sleep patterns, your overall health and your entire vocal system.

This condition, recognized by doctors as Temporomandibular Joint Disorders, (*TMJ or TMD Disorders*), is a problem or symptom of the chewing muscles and joints that connect your lower jaw to your skull. If you have a popping sound in the jaw or tense jaws upon waking up in the morning or clench your teeth at night, this indicates there is a chronic tension. Sometimes we just have this all our life, and must learn ways to manage it.

Dealing with any tensions in the jaw is challenging for the mind and the body. The more relaxed you can be before you begin with any corrective exercises, the better.

During the past twenty years that I've been teaching in Europe, Israel and America, I would say about 85% of the female singers I've taught have had some kind muscle tension in the jaw and chin. This goes for almost every level—from beginner to professional. This is particularly true for pop, jazz and rock singers, although I've seen this many times in my opera students as well.

The jaw muscle is frequently tense in today's culture due to a variety of causes. I am aware of several ways to improve serious problems with TMJ disorders such as corrective bio-esthetic dentistry, acupuncture, diet changes, or chiropractic adjustments. (*I've referred some of my students to several experts in these fields, with whom they have experienced positive results.*) In general, whether you have chronic TMJ issues or not, tensions in this area should not be ignored.

Daily stress and emotional upsets can also make the jaw area tense. Therefore, I give my students simple, individualized exercises that target the muscles of the jaw hinge along with other gentle breathing exercises, to reduce chronic or daily build-up of these kinds of stresses. While doing these exercises my students are encouraged to use a mirror and identify any distortions in face or posture that may be interfering with their singing.

Generally, I also advocate singing with the mouth in a Buddha like smile, but not a stiff or fixed smile. The lips should be able to relax, extend or even pout for certain notes. Students may be shown how to take a tiny yawn or gentle sigh as they sing descending tones. (You can also review some of the breath-release exercises in previous chapters.) The jaw hinge moves both up and down. Remember this when doing the exercises below.

Gentle Tension Release:
Level 1: Jaw Placement and Hint of a Yawn

Sit on a good chair in front of a mirror. Place feet firmly on the floor. For a moment, gently massage with light fingertips the jaw hinge right at your ears, and pause.

- Now, gently inhale and exhale several times with closed yet gently smiling mouth position.
- Close and open the mouth a tiny bit, doing so very slowly for a few times. Pause and repeat.
- Now open the mouth about one to two fingers wide, still feeling that tiny Buddha smile.
- Keeping the lower jaw stable, begin to yawn a little. Deepen the yawn just *a little*. Notice a *tiny lift upwards*, in your upper lips and jaw hinge.
- Repeat. Feel the air suspended lightly inside. Look in the mirror. Notice the position of your chin now. It should feel softer and not jut out.

Don't overdo this yawn sensation. Maintain the little smile, as the jaw also moves *up* just a bit. Your chin shouldn't go down more than an inch or two.

The great Swedish dramatic Wagnerian singer, Kirstin Flagstaff, was known to say that learning how to stay relaxed is an art that singers should master and that yawning often, and on purpose, helped her stay very calm and centered for the demanding Wagnerian dramatic soprano roles she sang.

The jaw muscles are strong. Now we use them to chew our food, but in ancient times, we also used our jaw muscles to rip and tear. The muscles around the jaw hinge must be trained to remain responsive to gentle movements of articulation and diction. Why?

If your jaw or chin jut out too much when you sing, particularly on high notes, or are overly stiff, this tenses up diction and articulation. Such tension freezes up the breath and closes off the throat. It's difficult to sing well, let alone to feel at ease singing this way. If you factor in normal nervous energy while performing combined with extra jaw tensions, singing can become a painful experience for you.

If you're holding and squeezing notes out, the emotion heard by the audience, despite all that is in your heart, may be a kind of whining, strident, anxious sort of sound. If that *is* the emotion you want to project through your voice, it becomes an artistic choice. However, if this kind of emotion is *all* you can do, it's time to recondition the muscles.

You could say that part of vocal training is learning how to keep your mouth slightly open, in a relaxed position for a long period of time. The entire diaphragmatic region will release and function better when the extra tensions in the jaw and chin are eliminated. Once this happens, the singer feels a tremendous sense of relief. The breath now flows over vowels into the resonant chambers of the face automatically.

For opera and classical music singers, too much tension in the jaw hinge and chin is a very serious issue. Musical theater, pop and belting singers can sing with more tensions there, but over time, this kind of stress if not managed can affect the quality of their singing. Always consider healthy vocal function first, before dealing with the needs of a specific vocal style.

Gentle Tension Release
Level 2: Buddha Smile, Sound and Movement

Stand tall, in front of a mirror. Shift your upper body a bit forward, over your hips. Assume the Buddha Smile and lower your head down just a tiny bit.

- Open your mouth just a little, about one finger wide. Observe what this looks like in the mirror.
- Keep the mouth small, and sigh out a long *Wu* then a long *Wee*. Repeat several times in a row.
- Now repeat *Wu* gliding into a *Wee* sound, moving the arms as if parting heavy curtains.
- Did you feel air opening the lower ribs *before* you sighed out the *Wu* or *Wee*?

Repeat the sequence three more times. Now, try out a phrase from a song or scale. What did you notice?

Releasing the jaw hinge from an overly tense position immediately relaxes the breathing system. All of these suggestions are part of a reconditioning process that is modified for the specific tensions and needs of each singer's voice.

CHAPTER 18

Challenges and Choices

We are coming to the final pages of this little book. I hope that by now you are fully convinced how special singing is and why you can never sound like a piano.

To feel that you were born to sing and receiving acclaim in this field, are not always one and the same. Many factors must come into place. For some women, a combination of talent, hard work and connections will give them an important career that rapidly develops. For others, the path will not be as smooth.

Becoming famous does not have to be the criteria for success. Many singers who are able to earn a decent living from their work consider themselves very successful. Still others may find that singing beautifully in choirs, their community or in special events brings them satisfaction. For others, becoming established as a respected voice teacher brings joy. The kind of singing career that develops depends on the woman — her aims and ambitions, personality, talent and destiny.

Today, singers can utilize an amazing array of technology that can create positive career opportunities along with bigger illusions about what it takes to sing. The same technology that may get you an audience on YouTube or TV also fuels a media industry that sells musical formulas and packaged entertainers. Commercial music is a big business. Within this matrix of powers and influences, many women singers can lose their sense of self-worth, autonomy and musical direction.

If the challenges we face as professional singers and voice teachers in today's competitive and changing music scene are often complex for us to handle, how much more so are they for those just starting out? The outward pressures and demands of the music industry, either in popular or classical music, continue to present us with issues about defining our audience and our message. Our path is not easy. However, as singers and educators we should not be dismayed by this. Instead, we must continue to define our creative ideals and keep our artistic goals in sight.

Choose music that you believe in and love. Without that conviction, you can't access your full vocal and musical potential. Through the power of that conviction, your talent and artistry will touch people's hearts and you will find your niche as a singer. Performing a song that you wrote, singing a beautiful aria, a cheerful musical theater song, a melancholy jazz tune, or an emotionally charged rock ballad can inspire the heart, bring joy to a party, lighten someone's sorrow or help them to forget their pain for a few hours.

No matter what musical style you sing, deciding to develop your singing talent and share it with others is a powerful choice to make. It changes your life. Not everyone will understand or support this decision. What is important, however, is what you do with your gift and how your safeguard it.

With a solid vocal method and ongoing studies, you should be able to perform and sing well into your sixties, or even longer. However, if your voice has changed significantly in power, or there is loss in the physical strength necessary to sustain singing night after night, you need to take care of that. If you have ongoing vocal weakness, the worst thing you can do is continue singing without getting some help. Don't sing when your vocal cords are red or swollen or if you are totally exhausted.

Remember, you are not a piano with strong metal strings. You are basing your career on those little vocal cords! Make adjustments to your schedule. Schedule time for vocal silence and rest, refreshing breaks with friends or doing activities that you enjoy aside from music.

Staying healthy and fit

If you want to sing well into your sixties or longer, you must really monitor the physical side of things such as maintaining a healthy diet, exercise, managing stress, allergies, and sufficient sleep. With all the pollution in our cities and our skies, there may also be upper-respiratory issues that need attention. However, try to avoid over-the-counter drugs, as they can become habit forming without necessarily treating the source of the problem. Daily vocal warm-ups of the kind discussed in earlier chapters can also keep your vocal cords healthy. These warm-ups naturally loosen phlegm on the chords. If you are still having chronic vocal issues, consult a good ENT doctor, naturopathic doctor or a holistic alternative medicine practitioner, before doing anything drastic.

We all want to look and feel good. Being on stage or in front of the public requires us to look and feel our best. Some excellent ways for singers to keep in shape would be 20 to 30 minutes of daily walking, or several times a week of dancing, *Pilates*, *Tai Chi*, *Chi Gung*, *Hatha Yoga*, *Anusara* or *Iyengar Yoga*, or *The Alexander Technique*. Even if you're not planning a professional singing career, these kinds of mind/body disciplines can help you to stay fit, remain youthful and keep your joints and muscles flexible. Generally, heavy weight lifting (which can overly tighten the neck/chest area) or high impact sports are not recommended for singers, but can be done moderately.

Changes in your voice and repertoire

As mentioned in earlier chapters, the female voice changes noticeably in the teen years. However, not only does it change during these years, but also during and after pregnancy, as well as in menopause. These hormonal effects are not always negative. The timbre and quality of your voice may become lighter or heavier during these times of change. However, if vocal function has significantly changed, you may simply need to return to doing basic *vocalizes* again and take time to adjust to this new voice. Changing musical keys higher or lower for some songs may be required, or even the style of music you sing. You may find yourself able to perform music that requires more vocal heft and is more dramatic, or conversely, shift into lighter roles. Therefore, remain musically and artistically open to new ideas, and be willing to make adjustments to suit your voice.

The longer we sing, the more we learn to respect our precious body that houses those two little vocal cords. Hopefully this will lead to learning how to maintain a healthy lifestyle and discovering how to create harmony, peace, love and joy in all that we do.

Staying sane in the business of music

Having a singing career can bring us many wonderful experiences. However, it can be a challenging and unconventional way to live. Whether you sing opera, musical theater or popular music, your work demands constant training and staying on top of your game. Your singing life may require a lot of traveling. Sometimes you are in shows or productions you absolutely love. You get along well with the cast and directors. Other times, conditions are more difficult.

To perform effectively, singers need to know how to protect their nerves, health and artistic intentions. We can be particularly vulnerable to the needs of our families, our spouses, children or partners. We want to nurture and give to our loved ones, but we also expend considerable energy maintaining our networks and developing the business of singing. All these types of demands can take their toll on us.

Therefore, it's important to find ways to stay positive, emotionally balanced and learn how to say the word "*No.*" Having the courage to do this is very liberating. You may need to say no (of course in a polite and charming way) to your manager or producer about certain business arrangements. You may decide against doing a musical production that you don't have time for or really believe in. You may need to limit socializing when preparing for a major new role or in the weeks during performances. On the week of a show, you should skip late night meetings, parties and eating foods that don't agree with you, or performing night after night without enough rest.

The opera scene today—what's going on?

Just as top popular singers with wonderful talent find themselves being pressured to perform in extravagant shows that may challenge their artistic sensibilities with disturbingly negative themes, opera singers, even the famous ones, face similar pressures.

Opera singers don't have the artistic influence over productions they had many decades ago. In those times, leading singers had more of a say in how their roles were staged, even traveling from company to company using costumes designed just for them. While many aspects of how opera is presented have changed, it is also becoming more popular. In part, this may be due to the success of HD Live operas seen in movie houses that are broadcast from major opera companies (*Metropolitan Opera, La Scala, LA Opera, etc.*), innovative staging, and clever marketing showcasing an abundance of well-trained, attractive, young and talented singers emerging from all over the globe.

A good thing to remember for those starting their opera career is that you may have a very different idea about how your role should be done, compared with what the directors or conductors have in mind. Therefore, remain flexible and innovative when you are in rehearsal, but don't be afraid to speak with either the conductor or the director if you need help with their approach.

Having performed internationally with a variety of opera companies as a mezzo-soprano soloist in updated or modernized opera productions, I am aware of the acting and artistic challenges this presents to a singer, especially when the opera's story or main characters may be rewritten by the stage director. For example, some directors' say they want more realism in the production, but don't provide dramatic logic in their staging, let alone minimal props that would enhance the characters' actions on stage.

The young opera singer may also feel uncomfortable reconciling the beautiful music they sing with what they have to do on stage. As in much of popular entertainment today, the trend of inserting gratuitous violence, sexuality and nudity into opera productions has increased. Each artist will need to find his or her own way in all of this.

What it's all for

Whether it's classical or contemporary, great music performed by great singers can heal and inspire. However, many global entertainment productions take the easy way out by evoking drama with facile methods like shock tactics, vulgarity and grime instead of conveying the range of human emotions through thought provoking music and performances. It's much easier to take the audience's breath away by sending someone onto the stage naked than with an intense musical delivery. Until those who are famous or influential in the business speak up or make changes in production values, these kinds of challenges will remain for performers and creative artists.

A measure of artistic control can be achieved by producing your own shows, collaborating with like-minded musicians, building a concert or recital career, or founding your own ensemble. Regardless of where you are going as a singer, it's important to have your own definition of success. This will help you deal with the inevitable ups and downs of being a singer.

However, no matter what kind of music you sing, whether it's musical theater, opera, world music, pop or jazz, keep in mind the love you have for music and why you chose to sing in the first place. For inspiration, we can also look to great artists of the past, such as the unforgettable dramatic soprano, Maria Callas, who brought new life to opera. In one of her TV interviews (which I paraphrase), she expressed her views about what it's all for, saying: "*I believe that in the theater, one goes – to see and feel something better than what we usually have in life. We have enough of miserable situations and things to cope with. When one leaves the theater, feeling improved, or breathes better, saying: 'Well that was something worth going for,'* **that** *I believe, is our main purpose. How we go about it, I don't care, as long as we succeed in that. And music is the straight way to go – to the heart – and to the minds of people.*"*

As long as there are talented women who want to master the art of singing and serve a higher purpose with their music, there is hope for all of us. They will be the ones who can carry forward the variety of great musical traditions that we, their teachers and mentors, strive to impart. My hope and wish for you is that you are one of those women.

Whatever music you sing, whether your audiences are large or small, have courage to study well, sing from the heart and aim high. Doing so will lead you to a profound experience, one that is worth the effort – of how vocal magic happens.

Closing Thoughts: The Song Within

Having vocal talent is a gift that comes with a responsibility. Deciding to become a singer can be a powerful expression of who you are and what you stand for. For your musical journey, choose the best team and expert guidance that you can.

How will we use our gifts? Can we bring to life the musical genius of great composers? Will the songs we write and perform bring hope and inspiration to our audiences, or put us deeper into ignorance and sleep?

What you choose to sing and promote with your music does matter. What does it mean for you?

Music can be a wonderful and faithful companion in life. I believe that great music performed by a gifted singer makes our lives infinitely better. I also believe that singing is the fastest road to spiritual bliss and just plain feeling happy.

In closing, my heartfelt wishes to you are these:

May you aspire to create something worth living for with your voice and music.
May you treasure your vocal gifts and find reward, not only in applause, but also in knowing that you have offered your best.

You possess great healing powers with your talent. As you discover your highest potential as a vocal artist, may the music you sing become the healing magic for your family, your friends and your world.

Recommended Reading:

Voice/Music Therapy, Audio-Linguistics, Diction, TMJ:

Alfred Tomatis:	The Ear and Language
	The Conscious Ear
Paul Maduale:	When Listening Comes Alive
Don Campbell:	Music and Miracles
	The Mozart Effect
	Music Physician
Daniel R. Boone:	The Voice and Voice Therapy
Randall McClellan:	The Healing Forces of Music
	History, Theory & Practice
Geoffrey G. Forward with Elisabeth Howard	American Diction for Singing
Dr. Jerry M. Simon	Stop Headaches Now
	Take the Bite out of Headaches

Great Opera Singers about Singing:

Lilli Lehman:	How to Sing
Caruso and Tetrazzini:	On the Art of Singing
Lillian Nordica:	Hints to Singers
Lotte Lehman:	More Than Singing:
	The Interpretation of Songs
Francis Alda:	Men, Women and Tenors
Eileen Farrell:	Can't Help Singing

Paraphrased Quote, Chapt.18: Maria Callas Interview
https://www.youtube.com/watch?v=MApX-iqCszs –
The Callas Conversations Volume One Part One 1968 (1)

ABOUT THE AUTHOR:

For over twenty years, **Ahdda Shur** has been empowering hundreds of female singers of all ages to find their vocal magic, whether they sing opera, musical theater, pop, jazz or sacred music.

A former international opera soloist singing in mezzo-soprano and soprano repertoire, she has also performed musical theater, recorded and performed sacred and world music. Critics have hailed her as "a *first-rate artist, with a fabulous voice,*" "*passionate and believable*" and "*a consummate musician.*"

She holds a Master's Degree in Opera Stage Direction from the Indiana University School of Music, Bloomington, and was Professor of Voice at the Levinsky College of Education, Tel Aviv, Israel; The New World School of the Arts, Miami, Florida; and at Barry University, Miami, Florida.

Ahdda Shur teaches from her private voice studio in Los Angeles, California. She is the creator of *Bel Canto with VOGA™: Voiceyoga for Peak Performances,* and also offers masterclasses and workshops about this method. **Sopranos Are Not Pianos** is her first book.

For the Free Bonuses in this book, and other information:

WWW.SHURVOICE.COM

Testimonials for Ahdda Shur's Vocal Coaching

"Ahdda was trained in the true Italian Bel Canto technique that gave us the great singers from Caruso to Callas…She brings contemporary techniques of mind/body awareness to bear on communicating the Bel Canto approach to the modern student." – **Dr. Douglas Lundeen, French Horn Soloist; Prof. of French Horn, Rutgers University, New Jersey**

"I warmly recommend Ahdda as a most delightful colleague, talented artist and teacher." – **Joy Davidson, mezzo-soprano opera soloist; former Head of Opera, New World School of the Arts, Miami, Florida**

"Ahdda…the producer said it was the best he had ever heard me sound! He was truly amazed. Thank you. It was so much fun and effortless to sing and record this time…" – **Lyssa Aya Trenier, pop singer & recording artist, New York, New York**

"…Ahdda helped me enormously with my singing technique…breathing and posture…diction [and was] able to diagnose the source of problems that had haunted my performances for years" – **Jen Ferro, musical theater & opera mezzo-soprano, Eugene, Oregon**

"In addition to Ahdda's expertise as a vocal coach and her VOGA™ voiceyoga methods, she brings her heart and soul into the work that she does. Ahdda's voice is from heaven…and has inspired me to find peace and balance within…" – **Marla Mervis-Hartmann, Actress; Living Light Reiki Master, Los Angeles, California**

"The results of Ahdda's work [with our two teenage daughters] have been nothing short of dramatic - their singing has improved greatly in a short period of time…" – **Joel Berman, parent, Los Angeles, California**

WWW.SHURVOICE.COM

www.ingramcontent.com/pod-product-compliance
Lightning Source LLC
Chambersburg PA
CBHW030142170426
43199CB00008B/165